First World War

and Army of Occupation

War Diary

France, Belgium and Germany

30 DIVISION
Headquarters, Branches and Services
Royal Army Veterinary Corps
Assistant Director Veterinary Services
16 November 1915 - 31 March 1919

WO95/2320/3

The Naval & Military Press Ltd
www.nmarchive.com
Published in association with The National Archives

Published by

The Naval & Military Press Ltd

Unit 10 Ridgewood Industrial Park,

Uckfield, East Sussex,

TN22 5QE England

Tel: +44 (0) 1825 749494

www.naval-military-press.com

www.nmarchive.com

This diary has been reprinted in facsimile from the original. Any imperfections are inevitably reproduced and the quality may fall short of modern type and cartographic standards.

Contents

Document type	Place/Title	Date From	Date To
Heading	Assistant Director Veterinary Services.		
Heading	30th Division Divl Troops D.A.D. Ordnance Services Nov 1915-Mar 1919		
Heading	D.A.D.O. 30th Div Vol I Nov 15 Mar 19		
War Diary	Ailly Le Haut Cloches	16/11/1915	17/11/1915
War Diary	Flesselles	18/11/1915	28/11/1915
War Diary	Fienvillers	29/11/1915	30/11/1915
Heading	D.A.D.O.S. 30th Division. Volume 1 November 1915 War Diary.		
Heading	D.A.D.O. 30th Div. Vol. 2		
War Diary	Fienvillers	01/12/1915	03/12/1915
War Diary	War Diary D.A.D.O.S. 30th Division. Volume 2 December 1915		
War Diary	Fienvillers	04/12/1915	31/12/1915
Heading	D.A.D.O. 30th Div. Vol. 3		
War Diary	Fienvillers	01/01/1916	14/01/1916
Heading	War Diary D.A.D.O.S. 30th Division 1st January 1916 To 14th January 1916		
War Diary	Etinehem	14/01/1916	31/01/1916
Heading	D.A.D.O.S. 30th Div. Vol. 4		
Heading	War Diary of D.A.D.O.S. 30th Div From 1st February 1916 To 29th February 1916		
War Diary	Etinehem	01/02/1916	29/02/1916
Heading	War Diary of D.A.D.O.S. 30th Divn. From 1st March 1916 To 31st March 1916 Vol 5		
War Diary	Etinehem	01/03/1916	20/03/1916
War Diary	Montigny	21/03/1916	23/03/1916
War Diary	Daours	24/03/1916	28/03/1916
War Diary	Ailly Sur Somme	29/03/1916	31/03/1916
Heading	War Diary of D.A.D.O.S. 30th Divn. from 1st April 1916 To 30th April 1916 Vol 6		
War Diary	Ailly Sur	01/04/1916	04/04/1916
War Diary	Ailly S/Somme	05/04/1916	30/04/1916
Heading	War Diary of D.A.D.O.S. 30th Div From 1st May 1916 to 31st May 1916		
War Diary	Ailly S/Somme	01/05/1916	05/05/1916
War Diary	Etinehem.	06/05/1916	31/05/1916
Heading	D.A.D.O.S. 30th Div Vol 8 June War Diary of D.A.D.O.S. 30th Div. from 1st June 1916 to 30th June 1916		
War Diary	Etinehem.	01/06/1916	30/06/1916
Heading	30 July 30 Div D.A.D.O.S. Vol. 9 War Diary of D.A.D.O.S. 30th Divn From July 1st 1916 to July 31st 1916		
War Diary	Etinehem	01/07/1916	01/07/1916
War Diary	Corbie	02/07/1916	22/07/1916
War Diary	F. 19. D.	23/07/1916	31/07/1916
Heading	D.A.D.O.S. Vol 10 War Diary of D.A.D.O.S. 30th Divn from to August 1st 1916 to Aug 31st 1916		
War Diary	F. 19. D.	01/08/1916	02/08/1916

War Diary	Hangest	03/08/1916	05/08/1916
War Diary	Bethune	06/08/1916	31/08/1916
Heading	War Diary of D.A.D.O.S. 30th Div From Sept 1st 1916 to Sept 30th 1916		
War Diary	Bethune	01/09/1916	19/09/1916
War Diary	Doullens	20/09/1916	21/09/1916
War Diary	Vignacourt	22/09/1916	30/09/1916
Heading	War Diary of D.A.D.O.S. 30th Div From 1st October 1916 to October 31st 1916		
War Diary	Vignacourt	01/10/1916	03/10/1916
War Diary	Ribemont	04/10/1916	14/10/1916
War Diary	E.10.D.1.1.	14/10/1916	26/10/1916
War Diary	Boquemaison	27/10/1916	31/10/1916
Heading	Vol 13 War Diary of D.A.D.O.S. 30th Divn. From Nov. 1st 1916 to Nov. 30th 1916		
War Diary	Bavincourt	01/11/1916	30/11/1916
Heading	War Diary of D.A.D.O.S. 30th Divn. From Dec 1st 1916 to Dec 31st 1916 Vol 14		
War Diary	Bavincourt	01/12/1916	31/12/1916
Heading	War Diary of D.A.D.O.S. 30th Div From 1st January 1917 to 31st January 1917 Vol 15		
War Diary	Bavincourt	01/01/1917	06/01/1917
War Diary	Lucheux	07/01/1917	31/01/1917
Heading	War Diary of D.A.D.O.S. 30th Divn. from Feb 1st 1917 to Feb 28th 1917 Vol 16		
War Diary	Lucheux	01/02/1917	05/02/1917
War Diary	Berneville	06/02/1917	28/02/1917
Heading	War Diary of D.A.D.O.S. 30th Div From 1st March 1917 to 31st March 1917 Vol 17		
War Diary	Berneville	01/03/1917	26/03/1917
War Diary	Bretencourt	27/03/1917	31/03/1917
Heading	War Diary of D.A.D.O.S. 30th Divn. from 1st April 1917 to 30 April 1917 Vol 18		
War Diary	Bretencourt	01/04/1917	13/04/1917
War Diary	Pommier	14/04/1917	20/04/1917
War Diary	Achicourt	21/04/1917	29/04/1917
War Diary	Roellecourt	30/04/1917	30/04/1917
Heading	War Diary of D.A.D.O.S. 30th Divn. From May 1st 1917 to May 31st 1917 Vol 19		
War Diary	Roellecourt	01/05/1917	03/05/1917
War Diary	Oeuf	04/05/1917	15/05/1917
War Diary	Willeman	16/05/1917	21/05/1917
War Diary	Pernes	22/05/1917	22/05/1917
War Diary	Norrent Fontes	23/05/1917	24/05/1917
War Diary	Steenbecque	25/05/1917	26/05/1917
War Diary	Wotau	27/05/1917	30/05/1917
War Diary	G.14. b.5.4	31/05/1917	31/05/1917
Heading	War Diary of D.A.D.O.S. 30th Divn. From 1st June 1917 to 30th June 1917 Vol 20		
War Diary	G.14. b.5.4	01/06/1917	14/06/1917
War Diary	G.34. b.8.10	15/06/1917	30/06/1917
Heading	War Diary of D.A.D.O.S. 30th Divn. From July 1st 1917 to July 31st 1917 Vol 21		
War Diary	G.34. b.8.10 (Reninghelst)	01/07/1917	07/07/1917
War Diary	Nordasques	08/07/1917	18/07/1917
War Diary	Steenvoorde	19/07/1916	24/07/1916

War Diary	Reninghelst	25/07/1916	31/07/1916
Heading	War Diary of D.A.D.O.S. 30th Div From August 1st 1917 to 31st August 1917 Vol 22		
War Diary	Reninghelst.	01/08/1917	05/08/1917
War Diary	Godwerswelde	06/08/1917	07/08/1917
War Diary	Merris	08/08/1917	11/08/1917
War Diary	St. Jans Cappel	12/08/1917	23/08/1917
War Diary	Dranoutre	24/08/1917	31/08/1917
Heading	War Diary of D.A.D.O.S. 30th Div From 1st Sept 1917 To 30th Sept 1917 Vol 23		
War Diary	Dranoutre	01/09/1917	30/09/1917
Heading	War Diary of D.A.D.O.S. 30th Div From 1st October 1917 to 31st October 1917 Vol 24		
War Diary	Dranoutre	01/10/1917	31/10/1917
Heading	War Diary of D.A.D.O.S. 30th Div From 1st Nov. 1917 to 30th Nov 1917 Vol 25		
War Diary	Dranoutre	01/11/1917	16/11/1917
War Diary	Steenvoorde	17/11/1917	26/11/1917
War Diary	Westoutre	27/11/1917	30/11/1917
Heading	War Diary of D.A.D.O.S. 30th Divn. from 1/12/17 to 31/12/17 Vol 26		
War Diary	Westoutre	01/12/1917	31/12/1917
Heading	War Diary of D.A.D.O.S. 30th Division From January 1st 1918-to January 31st 1918 Vol 27		
War Diary	Westoutre	01/01/1918	06/01/1918
War Diary	Blaringhem	07/01/1918	09/01/1918
War Diary	Corbie	10/01/1918	13/01/1918
War Diary	Nesle	14/01/1918	19/01/1918
War Diary	Ercheu.	20/01/1918	28/01/1918
War Diary	Chauny	29/01/1918	31/01/1918
War Diary	Ognes	01/02/1918	08/02/1918
War Diary	Ercheu.	09/02/1918	23/02/1918
War Diary	Ham	24/02/1918	25/02/1918
War Diary	Dury	26/02/1918	28/02/1918
Heading	War Diary of D.A.D.O.S. 30th Div From 1-3-18 to 31-3-18 Vol 29		
War Diary	Dury.	01/03/1918	31/03/1918
Heading	War Diary of D.A.D.O.S. 30th Div From 1.4.18 to 30.4.18 Vol 30		
War Diary	St. Valery S/S	01/04/1918	03/04/1918
War Diary	Proven	04/04/1918	08/04/1918
War Diary	Elvedinghe	09/04/1918	12/04/1918
War Diary	St Sixte	13/04/1918	17/04/1918
War Diary	St Jan de Biezen	18/04/1918	26/04/1918
War Diary	Broxeele	27/04/1918	30/04/1918
Heading	War Diary of D.A.D.O.S. 30th Div From 1st May 1918 to 31st May 1918 Vol 31		
War Diary	Broxeele	01/05/1918	16/05/1918
War Diary	Eu	17/05/1918	31/05/1918
Heading	War Diary of D.A.D.O.S., 30th Divn From 1st June 1918 to 30th June 1918 Vol 32		
War Diary	Eu	01/06/1918	20/06/1918
War Diary	Rue	21/06/1918	27/06/1918
War Diary	Eperlecques	28/06/1918	30/06/1918
Heading	War Diary of D.A.D.O.S. 30th Div From 1st July 1918 to 31st July 1918 Vol 33		

War Diary	Eperlecques	01/07/1918	08/07/1918
War Diary	Cassel	09/07/1918	31/07/1918
Heading	War Diary of D.A.D.O.S. 30th Div From 1st Aug 1918 to 31st Aug 1918 Vol 34		
War Diary	Cassel	01/08/1918	31/08/1918
Heading	War Diary of D.A.D.O.S. 30th Division From 1st September 1918 to 30th September 1918 Vol 35		
War Diary	Godewaersvelde	01/09/1918	30/09/1918
Heading	War Diary of D.A.D.O.S. 30th British Division From 1st October 1918 to 31st October 1918 Vol 36		
War Diary	Godewaersvelde	01/10/1918	01/10/1918
War Diary	La Clytte	02/10/1918	19/10/1918
War Diary	Wervicq (Q.27)	20/10/1918	24/10/1918
War Diary	Sterhoek	25/10/1918	31/10/1918
Heading	War Diary of D.A.D.O.S. 30th British Division From 1st November 1918 to 30th November 1918 Vol 37		
War Diary	Sterhoek	01/11/1918	03/11/1918
War Diary	Belleghem	04/11/1918	28/11/1918
War Diary	Blaringhem	29/11/1918	30/11/1918
Heading	War Diary of D.A.D.O.S. 30th British Division From 1st December 1918 to 31st December 1918 Vol 38		
War Diary	Blaringhem.	01/12/1918	31/12/1918
Heading	War Diary of D.A.D.O.S. 30th British Division From 1st January 1919 to 31st January 1919 Vol 39		
War Diary	Blaringhem.	01/01/1919	31/01/1919
Heading	War Diary of D.A.D.O.S. 30th British Division From 1st Feby. 1919 to 28th Feby 1919 Vol 40		
War Diary	Blaringhem	01/02/1919	21/02/1919
War Diary	St Omer	22/02/1919	28/02/1919
War Diary	Headquarters, Ostrohove Camp, Boulogne.	01/03/1919	31/03/1919

ASSISTANT
DIRECTOR
VETERINARY
SERVICES

30TH DIVISION

DIVL TROOPS

D.A.D.ORDNANCE SERVICES

NOV 1915-MAR 1919

D.A.D.O.S. 30th Div.

Vol I

121
7935

Nov 15
|
Mar 19

Instructions regarding War Diaries and Intelligence Summaries are contained in F. S. Regs., Part II. and the Staff Manual respectively. Title pages will be prepared in manuscript.

Army Form C. 2118.

WAR DIARY
or
~~INTELLIGENCE SUMMARY.~~

(Erase heading not required.)

D.A.D.O.S.
30TH DIVISION.

Place	Date	Hour	Summary of Events and Information	Remarks and references to Appendices
	November 1915			
Ailly le Haut Clocher	16th		Joined 30th Division the day previous from First Corps and took over the Duties of D.A.D.O.S. Heavy snow during night 16th–17th. Went off to Amiens with a lorry to purchase Soft Soap for use in horses hooves to prevent Snow balling. Lieut Rogers A.O.D left this morning for Calais.	
"	17th		Division moved to New Area.	
Flesselles	18th		System of Sending Stores to Brigade dumps started.	
"	19th		My predecessor had wired for 20000 tube helmets to make a Divisional Reserve of 1 per man, ought to have indented for Ordinary Pattern. Having arrived reported the matter to 3rd Army and was informed to put them in Store. Wired for 16000 blankets being the 2nd issue to other ranks.	
"	20th		Visited Railhead and found that the time spent by the Lorries waiting for Units at Dumps was too long which made the Offloading of trucks at Railhead very late.	
"	21st		Requested the Brigades to instruct their Units to call at the Ordnance dump at Flesselles for the future.	

2353 Wt. W2544/1454 700,000 5/15 D. D. & L. A.D.S.S. Forms/C. 2118.

Instructions regarding War Diaries and Intelligence Summaries are contained in F. S. Regs., Part II. and the Staff Manual respectively. Title pages will be prepared in manuscript.

WAR DIARY
or
~~INTELLIGENCE SUMMARY.~~
(Erase heading not required.)

D.A.D.O.S.
30TH DIVISION.

Army Form C. 2118.

Sheet 2

Place	Date	Hour	Summary of Events and Information	Remarks and references to Appendices
	November 1915			
Flesselles	22nd		Visited Head Quarters of 89th & 90th Brigades. Reported that the boots issued to the men just prior to proceeding oversees were very poor and that large numbers would be required. Went to Amiens in the afternoon purchasing	
"	23rd		Divisional Hd Qrs enquired what Periscopes were in possession of Infantry Units. Visited 91st Brigade HQ in the afternoon. More Complaints about boots.	
"	24th		Winter Clothing started to arrive today. Owing to hearing so many Complaints about bad boots wired to Base for 5000 pairs. Trying to obtain news of 2 Trucks which had been despatched from Paris with Horse rugs. Went to Longpré and was informed by RTO that they were at Hangest.	
"	25th		Representative arrived from 3rd Army to investigate the boot question. COO Base having reported receipt of previous days wire for 5000 pairs. Saw some men of 11th South Lancs Regt who had bad boots. Representative was shown reports of Units regarding the boots but apparently came to the conclusion that such a number as asked for were not required	

2353 Wt. W2544/1454 700,000 5/15 D. D. & L. A.D.S.S. Forms/C 2118.

Instructions regarding War Diaries and Intelligence Summaries are contained in F. S. Regs., Part II. and the Staff Manual respectively. Title pages will be prepared in manuscript.

WAR DIARY
or
~~INTELLIGENCE SUMMARY.~~
(Erase heading not required.)

Army Form C. 2118.

Sheet 3

D.A.D.O.S.
30TH DIVISION.

Place	Date	Hour	Summary of Events and Information	Remarks and references to Appendices
	November 1915			
Flesselles	25th		Went to Amiens in the afternoon purchasing.	
"	26th		Informed by 3rd Army that indent for 5000 pairs boots had been reduced to 2500 pairs.	
"	27th		The A.O.C personnel attached for duty with Brigades do not understand their duties more especially the system of bulk issue they all seem very slow in grasping the particular routine.	
"	28th		Very busy preparing books for details of bulk issues.	
Fienvillers	29th		Moved here this morning. Ordnance dump in a farm house back from the road, billet and office in same room, two rooms on ground floor for Stores, space quite insufficient. Left a W.O. at Flesselles to close down dump and send Stores on.	
"	30th		Went to Doullens purchasing. In the afternoon a fire was observed in roof of dump, broke out under the rafters, found that the outlet on top of chimney was covered over so that the heat and smoke came out through holes in the chimney underneath the roof, the men had started a fire on the ground floor	

2353 Wt. W2544/1454 700,000 5/15 D. D. & L. A.D.S.S./Forms/C 2118.

Instructions regarding War Diaries and Intelligence Summaries are contained in F. S. Regs., Part II. and the Staff Manual respectively. Title pages will be prepared in manuscript.

WAR DIARY
or
~~INTELLIGENCE SUMMARY.~~
(*Erase heading not required.*)

D.A.D.O.S.
30TH DIVISION.

Army Form C. 2118.

Sheet 41

Place	Date	Hour	Summary of Events and Information	Remarks and references to Appendices
	November 1915			
Fienvillers	30th		The village fire brigade consisting of one man in a helmet arrived after the fire was put out, very little damage done.	

H D Polglass Lieut
D.A.D.O.S.
30TH DIVISION

2353 Wt. W2544/1454 700,000 5/15 D. D. & L. A.D.S.S. Forms/C. 2118.

D.A.D.O.S.
30TH DIVISION.

Volume 1

November 1915

War Diary

Instructions regarding War Diaries and Intelligence Summaries are contained in F. S. Regs., Part II. and the Staff Manual respectively. Title pages will be prepared in manuscript.

WAR DIARY
or
~~INTELLIGENCE SUMMARY.~~
(Erase heading not required.)

D.A.D.O.S.
30TH DIVISION.

Army Form C. 2118.

Sheet 1

Place	Date	Hour	Summary of Events and Information	Remarks and references to Appendices
	December 1915			
Fienvillers	1st		Went to Doullens purchasing. Sent a Lorry to Pont Remy to collect Leather Jerkins from 36 Division. 4th Division are drawing 23000 of the Tube Smoke Helmets left at Flesselles. Sent a W.O. with 2 Lorries to distribute Leather Jerkins received from 36 Division to 3 Units and bring back balance. He informed me that he carefully checked the issue to the first two Units but handed the balance over to 3rd Unit without checking. Unit has 857 in Excess.	
"	2nd		Visited H.Q. 30th Division. Started Divisional Armourers, Shoemakers and Tailors workshops. Units of Division who had gone to another Area for training wiring for boots. Another error in issue of Leather Jerkins.	
"	3rd		Stoves Soyers arrived. Reported that after completing Infantry Units and allowing 75 per battery there was a surplus of 3580 Leather Jerkins in Store. In the afternoon went to Doullens purchasing. Visited Railhead and returned 60 bales Jerkins which had arrived but not required at present. Hastened outstanding bulk requirements of Winter Clothing, supplies very slow in arriving	

2353 Wt. W2544/1454 700,000 5/15 D. D. & L. A.D.S.S. Forms/C. 2118.

War Diary

D.A.D.O.S.
30TH DIVISION.

Volume 2
December
1915.

Instructions regarding War Diaries and Intelligence Summaries are contained in F. S. Regs., Part II. and the Staff Manual respectively. Title pages will be prepared in manuscript.

WAR DIARY
or
INTELLIGENCE SUMMARY.
(Erase heading not required.)

D.A.D.O.S.
30TH DIVISION.

Army Form C. 2118.

Sheet 2

Place	Date	Hour	Summary of Events and Information	Remarks and references to Appendices
	1915 December			
Fienvillers	4th		wired for 711[illegible] pairs boots. Reported that the Divisional Artillery had arrived. Went to Flesselles as 4th Division wired that there were still a large number of tube Helmets due to them, found by receipts given that actually 1400 had already been issued in excess. Units under the impression that I keep an Ordnance depôt and can supply anything in any quantity whenever they ask for it. 5 West Spring bomb throwers obtained from 3rd Army.	
"	5th		Units already complaining that they ought to be allowed to carry out their own repairs instead of sending boots &c to Divisional Shops	
"	6th		Visiting Units giving instruction in method of indenting for stores particularly bulk stores and checking Indents. Trying to get back copies of F.R.O's	
"	7th		Doullens in the afternoon Purchasing. Bulk indent to Base for 17300 steel Helmets. Complaint received from a Unit that the length of strap to a nose bag is too short. Sent a memo to each Unit having horses to submit their views. Called for a return of all Tents on charge of Units	
"	8th		Sent off a Lorry to R.E. Park for Bomb Throwers & Catapults, Lorry returned	

2353 Wt. W2544/1454. 700,000 5/15 D. D. & L. A.D.S.S. Forms/C. 2118.

Instructions regarding War Diaries and Intelligence Summaries are contained in F. S. Regs., Part II. and the Staff Manual respectively. Title pages will be prepared in manuscript.

WAR DIARY
or
~~INTELLIGENCE SUMMARY.~~
(Erase heading not required.)

Army Form C. 2118.

D.A.D.O.S.
30TH DIVISION.

Sheet 3

Place	Date	Hour	Summary of Events and Information	Remarks and references to Appendices
			Empty as they had already been issued to someone else. Lorry on return called at Rainneval and brought back 1 bass drum and 2 side drums left there by a Unit. 16 Rifles for Grenade firing received. One of the Sergeant Shoemakers in Divisional Shop could not agree with the others so had him exchanged. Wired to base for balance of Bomb Throwers and Catapults to complete to Scale. Had a conference of O.C. Batteries R.F.A (5 hours) Numerous Indents being received to replace losses.	
Treuvillers	9th		Submitted question of losses to Ad Qrs. Order published regarding same. Indents on Base for Dummy drill grenades. Went to Doullens Purchasing. All Units now in possession of Smoke Helmets and Antigas goggles. First receipt of Capes Mackintosh only 900 arrived. Lieut Liggett AOD arrived for instruction in Ordnance duties.	
"	10th		Units now completed with Magazines for Lewis Guns. Went to Amiens Purchasing. Called at Flexicourt to enquire about slag for the Ordnance Yard, inches of mud all over the place.	
"	11th		Sent to St Omer 4 lorries for slag. Leather for use in Divisional Shops	

2353 Wt. W2544/1454 700,000 5/15 D. D. & L. A.D.S.S. Forms/C. 2118.

Instructions regarding War Diaries and Intelligence Summaries are contained in F. S. Regs., Part II. and the Staff Manual respectively. Title pages will be prepared in manuscript.

WAR DIARY or ~~INTELLIGENCE SUMMARY.~~

(Erase heading not required.)

D.A.D.O.S. 30TH DIVISION.

Army Form C. 2118.

Sheet 4

Place	Date	Hour	Summary of Events and Information	Remarks and references to Appendices
	1915 December			
			not having arrived hastened same. No 010716 Pte H. Stevens AOC arrived for duty. Wired for 7537 pairs of boots. Interviewed O.C's of Batteries (7 hours) and (7 hours) with their Q.M. Sgts.	
Frenvillers	12		Lieut Leggett A.O.D left for duty as R.O.O at Geziancourt	
"	13		To Flexicourt to obtain Canvas for making Latrine Screens for a Field Ambulance. Lieut Stewart AOD arrived this day for instruction in Ordnance duties.	
"	14		Major Jones A.O.D. arrived to take over duties of D.A.D.O.S.	
"	15		Wired for bulk issue of 40 Vermoral Sprayers.	
"	"		Major Jones AOD left the Division this day for elsewhere. Artillery now seem to be under the impression that Stocks are maintained in the Field. Everything seem to be required at once. Went to Amiens Purchasing. Called on Units for a return showing Range Finders &c on charge	
"	16		Artillery seem to be in possession of poor boots as urgent indents are coming in. Spent the afternoon with an Artillery Brigade giving instruction. Went to Amiens Purchasing	

2353 Wt. W2544/1454 700,000 5/15 D. D. & L. A.D.S.S. Forms/C 2118.

Instructions regarding War Diaries and Intelligence Summaries are contained in F. S. Regs., Part II. and the Staff Manual respectively. Title pages will be prepared in manuscript.

WAR DIARY
or
~~INTELLIGENCE SUMMARY.~~
(Erase heading not required.)

Army Form C. 2118.

D.A.D.O.S.
30TH DIVISION.

Sheet 5

Place	Date	Hour	Summary of Events and Information	Remarks and references to Appendices
	1915 December			
Fienvillers	17		To Amiens purchasing. Wired for 5000 pairs Socks as a Divisional Reserve.	
"	18		Visited several Units in the morning. To Amiens in the afternoon to obtain a Sewing Machine for Workshops. Notified that the A.O.C. Staff of 91st Brigade will remain and join the 21st Brigade. Wired for 954 pairs boots. Wired for a Motor Car Rug required by Divisional Commander on payment.	
"	19		All day visiting Units adjusting queries and checking outstanding indents. Bulk Indent to Base for 5300 Leather Jerkins to complete Division.	
"	20		Visited D.O.M. 13th Corps to make arrangements for repairs and alterations to Water Carts. D.O.M. can carry out the work provided Units sending vehicles can send certain workmen with them do not think this at all likely. To Amiens in the afternoon purchasing had difficulty in finding a place where dubbing could be obtained however can obtain in any quantity from Paul Butard at about	

2353 Wt. W2544/1454 700,000 5/15 D. D. & L. A.D.S.S./Forms/C. 2118.

Army Form C. 2118.

Instructions regarding War Diaries and Intelligence Summaries are contained in F. S. Regs., Part II. and the Staff Manual respectively. Title pages will be prepared in manuscript.

WAR DIARY
or
~~INTELLIGENCE SUMMARY~~

(Erase heading not required.)

D.A.D.O.S.
30TH DIVISION. Sheet 6

Place	Date	Hour	Summary of Events and Information	Remarks and references to Appendices
	1915 December			
Fienvillers	20th		the same as Vocabulary rate. Authority received to issue bicycles to Artillery Units to replace horses (1 per Unit at present).	
"	21st		Sent a lorry to Amiens for 200 Kilos of Dubbing. Spent the morning with DAQMG 30 Division visiting regular battalions who had joined this Division to enquire into the state of their Equipment. Wired 89th Infy Bde to hasten Units to remove stores.	
"	22nd		Completed regular battalions, state of Equipment seem fair, complaints re boots, considered very poor quality. Went to Flexicourt to obtain quotation for rifle covers firm informed me that a reply would be sent in a few days as the question would have to be gone into. Firm in question is the largest makers of canvas in the North but business methods are very slow, ought to have named price on the spot.	
"	23rd		All day at Amiens purchasing.	
"	24th		Sent stores which had arrived for units, lately transferred to 7th Division, to D.A.D.O.S. War Office called for 20 pairs boots which Units had complained about. 1050 Capes Mackintosh arrived. Still 14000 due to	

2353 Wt. W2544/1454 700,000 5/15 D. D. & L. A.D.S.S. Forms/C. 2118.

Instructions regarding War Diaries and Intelligence Summaries are contained in F. S. Regs., Part II. and the Staff Manual respectively. Title pages will be prepared in manuscript.

WAR DIARY
or
~~INTELLIGENCE SUMMARY~~. D.A.D.O.S. 30TH DIVISION.

(Erase heading not required.)

Army Form C. 2118.

Sheet 7

Place	Date	Hour	Summary of Events and Information	Remarks and references to Appendices
	December 1915			
Heuvillers	24th		complete the Division To Amiens in the afternoon purchasing	
"	25th		Wired for 1622 pairs boots.	
"	26th		Supplementary wire sent for 786 pairs boots. Representative of a Unit called and stated that at least 400 pairs boots were required, Head Quarters of the Brigade sent a message that only 148 pairs were wanted while the Unit sent an Indent for but 75 pairs ? what number of boots did this particular Unit require.	
"	27th		Wired for special forges for use with petrol blow lamp. C.O.O called for a copy of the authority re DDOS 095/1. Balance of personnel required to complete Workshops should have reported for duty previous day but none up to present. Units very slow in replying to questions, have wired several times to two Units but no response, reported matter to Hd Qrs 30 Division. Wired Base for a sample Hyposcopic rifle rest for night firing, reply Cancelled article not known. Similar articles were issued for trial in First Corps months ago. Went to Amiens purchasing	

2353 Wt. W2544/1454 700,000 5/15 D. D. & L. A.D.S.S./Forms/C. 2118.

Instructions regarding War Diaries and Intelligence Summaries are contained in F. S. Regs., Part II. and the Staff Manual respectively. Title pages will be prepared in manuscript.

WAR DIARY
or
~~INTELLIGENCE SUMMARY.~~

(Erase heading not required.)

Army Form C. 2118.

D.A.D.O.S. 30TH DIVISION.

Sheet 8

Place	Date	Hour	Summary of Events and Information	Remarks and references to Appendices
	December 1915			
Frenvillers	28		Went to Amiens and bought 15 bends of Sole leather, no heel or toe tips or hob nails to be obtained. Various Units requested to send Vehicles which require alteration to D.O.M. Tradesmen such as Fitters, Blacksmiths or Carpenters seem to be very scarce in this Division majority of Units asked but very few obtainable. Wired for 15 Maxim Guns and 15 Tripod Mountings required to replace a similar number with Regular Battalions and condemned by Senior D.O.M. 15th Corps. Carriers hand Grenade to complete Units arrived.	
"	29		Notified Hd qrs 30 Division that 20 pairs of boots had been collected and were available for War Office who required same for inspection These were part of the boots complained about. Still trying to get a reply from an Artillery Unit, original request sent on 15th inst. Asked several Units to return 20 pairs bad boots, date and place of issue to be shown on a label attached to each pair, boots received but necessary information lacking. One lot of boots had on labels but the only thing on that was a mans regimental number and	

2353 Wt. W2544/1454 700,000 5/15 D. D. & L. A.D.S.S./Forms/C. 2118.

Army Form C. 2118.

Instructions regarding War Diaries and Intelligence Summaries are contained in F. S. Regs., Part II. and the Staff Manual respectively. Title pages will be prepared in manuscript.

WAR DIARY
or
INTELLIGENCE SUMMARY.

(Erase heading not required.)

D.A.D.O.S. 30TH DIVISION. Sheet 9

Place	Date	Hour	Summary of Events and Information	Remarks and references to Appendices
	December 1915			
Henvillers	29th		Name. Supplementary wire for 400 pairs boots for a Unit just returned from the front line. Numerous indents being continually received for unauthorized Stores, apparently Units do not read D.R.O.s, that DADOS of a Division cannot authorize Excess issues. Several indents received for assorted sizes of horse shoes. Purchasing stores at Amiens in the afternoon	
"	30th		Visiting Units regarding method of Submitting Indents and Settling queries with them.	
"	31st		Checking outstanding Indents with Units copies. Making out Fasteners finished up the Old Year working and started the New Year the Same.	

H D Polglase Captain
D.A.D.O.S.
30TH DIVISION.

2353 Wt. W2544/1454 700,000 5/15 D. D. & L. A.D.S.S. Forms/C 2118.

D.A.D.S. 30th Div:
Vol: 3

WAR DIARY
~~or~~
~~INTELLIGENCE~~ SUMMARY.
(*Erase heading not required.*)

Instructions regarding War Diaries and Intelligence Summaries are contained in F. S. Regs., Part II. and the Staff Manual respectively. Title pages will be prepared in manuscript.

Army Form C. 2118.

D.A.D.O.S. 30th Div.

Sheet 1

Place	Date	Hour	Summary of Events and Information	Remarks and references to Appendices
	January 1916			
Frenvillers	1st		No Truck from Base. Held 2 Conferences one with Quartermasters and Quartermaster Sergeants of 90th Brigade in the morning and one with the Quartermasters of the 89th Infy Brigade in the afternoon. All Units seem report that the mens boots are very poor quality. Up to date 12000 pairs issued which gives an average of 2000 pairs per week. Despatched 20 pairs to Base under instructions of War Office. These boots were issued in England and taken into Use just prior to Embarkation on 5. 11. 15.	
Frenvillers	2nd		Several Units arrived during the day for boots, issue made as far as possible from both new and repaired ones. Went with D A Q M G 30th Division to Etinehem to arrange Ordnance Dump and Divisional Workshops. Sent a Lorry to Bertrancourt for 6 cases Steel helmets left there by 17 Liverpool Regt. Had 2 Lorries going round the Area picking up Stoves Soyers Bomb throwers and Braziers from Units who were removing to new area. No truck from Base	
"	3rd		Visited A.D.O.S 13th Corps. In the afternoon went to Amiens purchasing.	
"	4th		Spent the morning with Store Staff preparing issues for Units who are on the	

2353 Wt. W2544/1454 700,000 5/15 D. D. & L. A.D.S.S. Forms/C. 2118.

Army Form C. 2118.

Instructions regarding War Diaries and Intelligence Summaries are contained in F. S. Regs., Part II. and the Staff Manual respectively. Title pages will be prepared in manuscript.

WAR DIARY
or
~~INTELLIGENCE SUMMARY~~
(Erase heading not required.)

Sheet 2

Place	Date	Hour	Summary of Events and Information	Remarks and references to Appendices
Frenvillers	4th		the new area. A.D.O.S. 13th Corps visited Dump, had one of the Brigade Acting W.O.'s in front of him for carelessness in his work. Visited Flexicourt to obtain samples of Canvas for making trench water carriers also went on to Ordnance 9th Division for some Periscopes for Grenade School.	
Frenvillers	5th		Visited A.D.O.S 13th Corps, Field Cashier and SOM 13th Corps in the morning. Went to Amiens in the afternoon purchasing.	
"	6th		Sent 2 Lorries with Stores for Units who had gone to New Area. In the afternoon went to Chipilly and Etinhem to try and arrange for a temporary building for an advanced Dump, no place available.	
"	7th		Hd Qrs 30th Division re Dump. As no place available until 12th inst. propose to send 2 Lorries every other day. At Dump ~~all~~ balance of day	
"	8th		Went to Flexicourt for Canvas for making trench water bags.	
"	9th		At dump all day assisting Brigade W.O.'s and instructing a Temporary Officer	
"	10th		Sent 2 lorry loads of Stores to Divisional Units. Went to 30th Division Head Quarters & was informed that Captn Malty was detailed to take over the Division as D.A.D.O.S and that I was to report as early as possible for duty	

Instructions regarding War Diaries and Intelligence Summaries are contained in F. S. Regs., Part II. and the Staff Manual respectively. Title pages will be prepared in manuscript.

WAR DIARY
or
~~INTELLIGENCE SUMMARY.~~
(Erase heading not required.)

Army Form C. 2118.

Sheet 3

Place	Date	Hour	Summary of Events and Information	Remarks and references to Appendices
Frenvillers	10th		with D.D.O.S. L of C. At Amiens purchasing. Capt Malty A.O.D arrived in the evening	
"	11th		Went with Capt Maltby to Divisional H.Q. To Elenheim to arrange with DADOS 5th Division about taking over Stores and Divisional Workshops.	
			Sent 2 lorry loads of Stores to Divisional Units.	
"	12th		Sent 11 lorry loads of Stores to new area also the whole of the AOD Divisional Staff with the exception of 2 men.	
"	13th		Sent balance of Stores to new area.	
"	14th		Sent 2 men to New Area. Closed Imprest account and handed over the same with balance of cash to Lt Stewart A.O.D. Reported for duty with D.D.O.S. L of C at Abbeville.	

H.D. Polglase Captain
DADOS 30th Division

T2134. Wt. W708–776. 500000. 4/15. Sir J. C. & S.

War Diary

D.A.D.O.S.
30th Division

1st January 1916
to
14th January 1916.

Instructions regarding War Diaries and Intelligence Summaries are contained in F. S. Regs., Part II. and the Staff Manual respectively. Title pages will be prepared in manuscript.

WAR DIARY
or
INTELLIGENCE SUMMARY.
(Erase heading not required.)

Army Form C. 2118.

Place	Date	Hour	Summary of Events and Information	Remarks and references to Appendices
Elinchem	14/1/16		Took over duties of DADOS from Capt H D Edglass AOD. Visited Railhead & distributed stores to troops	Wh.
Elinchem	15/1/16		Visited railhead & distributed stores to troops. Lectured the AOC staff of Brigade Groups regarding their duties, and took steps to arrange for necessary records to be kept with a view of organizing method of demand & supply of Ordnance Stores and of keeping necessary information so that the general situation of units' equipment is at all times known.	Wh.
Elinchem	16/1/16		Visited Railhead & distributed stores to troops. Commenced to dispose of accumulation of surplus stores. Continued lectures as on the 15th instant. Lectured all Qr Mrs of Infantry Units and Company QMS's &c on method of supply of Ordnance Stores in the field	Wh.
Elinchem	17/1/16		Visited Railhead & distributed stores to troops.	Wh.
Elinchem	18/1/16		Sent representative to railhead to take over stores. These were afterwards distributed to troops. Wired to Base for strips for QF 18 pr. fuze indicators required as Batteries are in possession of No 85 fuzes only.	Wh.
Elinchem	19/1/16		Stores arrived from Railhead & issued to troops. Purchased 1 Combined wringer and mangle & 2 Polo rubber wringers for use in Divisional Baths.	Wh.

2353 Wt. W2544/1454 700,000 5/15 D. D. & L. A.D.S.S./Forms/C. 2118.

Army Form C. 2118.

Instructions regarding War Diaries and Intelligence Summaries are contained in F. S. Regs., Part II. and the Staff Manual respectively. Title pages will be prepared in manuscript.

WAR DIARY
or
INTELLIGENCE SUMMARY.

(Erase heading not required.)

Place	Date	Hour	Summary of Events and Information	Remarks and references to Appendices
Ekneham	20/1/16		Stores arrived from Railhead & issued to troops	Wh.
Ekneham	21/1/16		Stores arrived from Railhead & issued to troops. Received 40 metal food warmers for issue to troops.	Wh.
Ekneham	22/1/16		Stores arrived from Railhead & issued to troops	Wh.
Ekneham	23/1/16		Stores arrived from Railhead & issued to troops. 18 Carriages Ambulance Stretcher arrived & issued to Field Ambulances. These complete the 20 allowed per Division	Wh.
Ekneham	24/1/16		Stores arrived from Railhead & issued to troops. Received notification that Divisional reserve of smoke helmets was in future to be 5000 of the Tube Pattern, and that reserve of ordinary pattern would be returned to Base on receipt of the tube pattern. 5000 Tube Pattern helmets demanded by wire	Wh.
Ekneham	25/1/16		Stores arrived from Railhead & issued to troops. Received instructions to demand Lewis guns for 4 Regular Infantry Bns in place of Maxim & Vickers in possession. Also to demand transport required for formation of 1 Bde Machine Gun for 21st Infantry Brigade	Wh. Wh.
Ekneham	26/1/16		Stores arrived from Railhead & issued to troops	Wh.
Ekneham	27/1/16		Stores arrived from Railhead & issued to troops	Wh.
Ekneham	28/1/16		Stores arrived from Railhead & issued to troops	Wh.

Instructions regarding War Diaries and Intelligence Summaries are contained in F. S. Regs., Part II. and the Staff Manual respectively. Title pages will be prepared in manuscript.

WAR DIARY
or
INTELLIGENCE SUMMARY.
(Erase heading not required.)

Army Form C. 2118.

Place	Date	Hour	Summary of Events and Information	Remarks and references to Appendices
Etinehem	29/1/16		Visited Railhead & distributed stores to troops. Demanded by wire 7000 Tube pattern smoke helmets to replace others exposed to gas	Wh.
Etinehem	30/1/16		Stores arrived from railhead & issued to troops	Wh.
Etinehem	31/1/16		Stores arrived from railhead & issued to troops. Wired for 800 smoke helmets for horses – 10% of establishment of horses as ordered.	Wh.

Whalley Capt.
DADOS
30th Division.

2353 Wt. W2544/1454 700,000 5/15 D. D. & L. A.D.S.S./Forms/C. 2118.

D.A.D.O.S. 30th Div

Vol: 4

Instructions regarding War Diaries and Intelligence Summaries are contained in F. S. Regs., Part II. and the Staff Manual respectively. Title pages will be prepared in manuscript.

WAR DIARY

~~or~~

~~INTELLIGENCE SUMMARY.~~

(Erase heading not required.)

Army Form C. 2118.

Place	Date	Hour	Summary of Events and Information	Remarks and references to Appendices
			Confidential War Diary of D.A.D.O.S. 30th Div. From 1st February 1916. To 29th February 1916	

2353 Wt. W2544/1454 700,000 5/15 D. D. & L. A.D.S.S./Forms/C. 2118.

Army Form C. 2118.

Instructions regarding War Diaries and Intelligence Summaries are contained in F. S. Regs., Part II. and the Staff Manual respectively. Title pages will be prepared in manuscript.

WAR DIARY
or
INTELLIGENCE SUMMARY.
(Erase heading not required.)

Place	Date	Hour	Summary of Events and Information	Remarks and references to Appendices
Etinehem	1 2/16		Stores arrived from Railhead & distributed to troops. Purchased locally 1 Forge and 1 Anvil for 17th Manchester Regt for shoeing purposes.	Wh.
Etinehem	2 2/16		Stores arrived from Railhead & distributed to troops. Lt D.R. Smith A.O.D. arrived for instruction from England	Wh.
Etinehem.	3 2/16		Stores arrived from Railhead & distributed to troops	Wh.
Etinehem	4 2/16		Stores arrived from Railhead & issued to troops.	Wh.
Etinehem	5 2/16		Stores arrived from Railhead & distributed to troops	Wh.
Etinehem	6 2/16		Stores arrived from Railhead & distributed to troops. Withdrew all ordinary smoke helmets held as a "reserve" for return to the Base. This leaves an authorised reserve of 5000 Tube Pattern Smoke Helmets.	Wh.
Etinehem	7 2/16		Stores arrived from Railhead & distributed to troops	Wh.
Etinehem	8 2/16		No stores arrived today for troops	Wh.
Etinehem	9 2/16		Stores arrived from Railhead & issued to troops	Wh.
Etinehem	10 2/16		Stores arrived from Railhead & issued to troops	Wh.
Etinehem	11 2/16		Stores arrived from Railhead & issued to troops. Handed over duties of D.A.D.O.S. to Lt A.G.B. Stewart A.O.D. Whalley Capt A.O.D. 11 2-16.	Wh.

Instructions regarding War Diaries and Intelligence Summaries are contained in F. S. Regs., Part II. and the Staff Manual respectively. Title pages will be prepared in manuscript.

WAR DIARY
or
INTELLIGENCE SUMMARY.
(Erase heading not required.)

Army Form C. 2118.

Sheet [illegible]

Place	Date	Hour	Summary of Events and Information	Remarks and references to Appendices
Etinehem	12/2/16		Stores arrived from Railhead & issued to Troops. Taken over duties of D.A.D.O.S. as from yesterday	AWD.
Etinehem	13/2/16		Stores arrived from Railhead, distributed to troops	AWD
Etinehem	14/2/16		No stores arrived today for troops	AWD
Etinehem	15/2/16		Stores arrived from Railhead, distributed to troops. Maxim gun arrived at Railhead for 21st Bde machine gun Co.	AWD
Etinehem	16/2/16		Stores arrived from Railhead, distributed to troops	AWD
Etinehem	17/2/16		Stores arrived from Railhead, distributed to Troops. Attended Court martial of 5906 Pte A W Taylor & gave evidence of his disobedience of orders given him by 02811 Staff Sergeant Wheatley	AWD
Etinehem	18/2/16		Stores arrived from Railhead, distributed to Troops	AWD
Etinehem	19/2/16		Stores arrived from Railhead, distributed to Troops	AWD.
Etinehem	20/2/16		Stores arrived from Railhead & distributed to Troops. Owing to the state of the roads the lorries from today will go to Railhead at night park there for the night, load up the Stores & will not be brought to the dump until after dark, when, after unloading they will proceed at once back to rail head.	AWD
Etinehem	21/2/16		Cond^r White, the chief clerk ordered to hospital with heart complaint. Stores arrived from railhead & got ready for distribution to Troops for the following day.	AWD

Instructions regarding War Diaries and Intelligence Summaries are contained in F. S. Regs., Part II. and the Staff Manual respectively. Title pages will be prepared in manuscript.

WAR DIARY
or
INTELLIGENCE SUMMARY.
(Erase heading not required.)

Army Form C. 2118.

Sheet 3

Place	Date	Hour	Summary of Events and Information	Remarks and references to Appendices
Etinehem	22/2/16		A/Sub/Cdr. Baader from 7th Division arrived for temporary duty to replace Cdr White. Stores arrived from Railhead got ready for distribution for the following day. System working very well. Placed No 04878 Pte J Howard under arrest for drunkeness whilst on active service. Stores arrived from Railhead at 10.15 pm.	APD
Etinehem	23/2/16		Stores arriving last night have been distributed to Troops. Wired to Base for two additional Lewis guns per Battn of this division under 3rd Army authority. Stores arrived from Railhead	APD
Etinehem	24/2/16		Stores arriving from Railhead last night have been distributed to Troops. No 04878 Pte Howard has this day been awarded 28 days Field Punishment No. 2 for drunkeness, by the Camp Commandant. Stores arrived from Railhead, experienced great difficulty on account of the state of the roads caused by heavy snowfall	APD.
Etinehem	25/2/16		Stores arriving last night have been distributed to Troops.	APD.
Etinehem	26/2/16		Stores arriving last night have been distributed to Troops. Visited Amiens in afternoon and carried out various purchases of stores for Troops. Indented on Base for 25000 P.H. Helmets to replace the P. Pattern Helmets. 26 Lewis guns have arrived & are being distributed to Battalions on the scale of 2 per Battn making them now in possession of 6 per Battn	APD.
Etinehem	27/2/16		Stores arriving from Railhead last night have been distributed to Troops. Detailed Pte Hiscock AOC to attend Photo School at III Army Headquarters for instruction in Helmets Antigas.	APD
Etinehem	28/2/16		Stores arriving from Railhead last night have been distributed to Troops.	APD

2353 Wt. W2544/1454 700,000 5/15 D. D. & L. A.D.S.S./Forms/C. 2118.

Instructions regarding War Diaries and Intelligence Summaries are contained in F. S. Regs., Part II. and the Staff Manual respectively. Title pages will be prepared in manuscript.

WAR DIARY
or
INTELLIGENCE SUMMARY.
(Erase heading not required.)

Army Form C. 2118.

Place	Date	Hour	Summary of Events and Information	Remarks and references to Appendices
Etinehem	29/3/16		Stores arriving last night from Railhead have been distributed to Troops. Visited Amiens in afternoon & purchased Stores urgently required by Troops. 2 Strombos Horns arrived from Base. These are used for giving warning, by a blast (which lasts for one minute) of an attack by gas.	APM
			APM —— Lieut AOD DADOS 30 Divn	

2353 Wt. W2541/1454 700,000 5/15 D. D. & L. A.D.S.S./Forms/C. 2118.

Instructions regarding War Diaries and Intelligence Summaries are contained in F. S. Regs., Part II. and the Staff Manual respectively. Title pages will be prepared in manuscript.

WAR DIARY
or
INTELLIGENCE SUMMARY.
(*Erase heading not required.*)

Army Form C. 2118.

Place	Date	Hour	Summary of Events and Information	Remarks and references to Appendices
			Confidential	DADOS 30th Div Vol. 5
			War Diary of D.A.D.O.S. 30th Divn	
			From 1st March 1916 to 31st March 1916.	

2353 Wt. W2544/1454 700,000 5/15 D. D. & L. A.D.S.S./Forms/C. 2118.

Instructions regarding War Diaries and Intelligence Summaries are contained in F. S. Regs., Part II. and the Staff Manual respectively. Title pages will be prepared in manuscript.

WAR DIARY
or
INTELLIGENCE SUMMARY.
(Erase heading not required.)

1st Sheet –

Army Form C. 2118.

Place	Date	Hour	Summary of Events and Information	Remarks and references to Appendices
Etinehem	1/3/16		Stores arriving from Railhead last night were distributed to troops – { This division is now in 4th Army from today –	APMS.
Etinehem	2/3/16		Stores arriving from Railhead last night were distributed to troops	APMS
Etinehem	3/3/16		Lorries may again use the roads from Railhead to Etinehem in daytime so stores are now distributed the same day as they arrive. as has been the case today. Visited Amiens in afternoon & carried out purchases of stores for troops.	APMS
Etinehem	4/3/16		Stores arrived from Railhead & distributed to troops.	APMS
Etinehem	5/3/16		No truck today.	APMS
Etinehem	6/3/16		Stores arrived from Railhead & distributed to troops	APMS
Etinehem	7/3/16		Stores arrived from Railhead & distributed to troops. Visited Amiens in the morning & purchased stores for the troops. including acetylene lamps hurricane for C.R.A	[illegible] APMS
Etinehem	8/3/16		Stores arrived from Railhead & distributed to troops.	APMS
Etinehem	9/3/16		Four Maxim guns handed over by QVR to 21st Infy. Bde returned to Base. in accordance with Q.O.S./142/5A. Stores arrived from Railhead & distributed to troops.	APMS
Etinehem	10/3/16		Stores arrived from Railhead & distributed to troops. Visited Amiens in afternoon & carried out purchase of stores for the Division	APMS

2353 Wt. W2544/1454 700,000 5/15 D. D. & L. A.D.S.S./Forms/C. 2118.

Instructions regarding War Diaries and Intelligence Summaries are contained in F. S. Regs., Part II. and the Staff Manual respectively. Title pages will be prepared in manuscript.

WAR DIARY
or
INTELLIGENCE SUMMARY.
(Erase heading not required.)

Army Form C. 2118.

2nd Sheet

Place	Date	Hour	Summary of Events and Information	Remarks and references to Appendices
Elinchem	11/3/16		Stores arrived from Railhead & distributed to Troops	apm
Elinchem	12/3/16		Stores arrived from Railhead & distributed to Troops. The new P.H. Helmets were included in todays trucks & will be issued in lieu of P Helmets. one helmet only being exchanged for the present	apm
Elinchem	13/3/16		Stores arrived from Railhead & distributed to Troops	apm
Elinchem	14/3/16		Stores arrived from Railhead & distributed to Troops. Condr. White returned from Home after dental treatment but he having been replaced by Condr. Baader his services are no longer required & ~~his~~ instructions as to his disposal have been asked for. Visited DADOS 18th Divn. at Montigny in connection with the move of this Division into the 18th Divn area	apm
Elinchem	15/3/16		Stores arrived from Railhead & issued to the Troops. Hotchkiss Gun arrived for Divisional Cavalry (~~D~~ 1/1st Lancashire Hussars D Squadron, but it is not being issued at present under Q instructions	apm
Elinchem	16/3/16		Stores arrived from Railhead & issued to the Troops.	apm
Elinchem	17/3/16		Stores arrived from Railhead & issued to the Troops. Visited Amiens in afternoon for purchase of Stores for the Troops	apm

2353 Wt. W2544/1454 700,000 5/15 D. D. & L. A.D.S.S./Forms/C. 2118.

Instructions regarding War Diaries and Intelligence Summaries are contained in F. S. Regs., Part II. and the Staff Manual respectively. Title pages will be prepared in manuscript.

WAR DIARY
or
INTELLIGENCE SUMMARY.
(Erase heading not required.)

3rd Sheet

Army Form C. 2118.

Place	Date	Hour	Summary of Events and Information	Remarks and references to Appendices
Etinehem	18/3/16		Stores arrived from Railhead issued to Troops.	A.M.
Etinehem	19/3/16		Cancelled trucks from Base for 3 days. owing to move. Visited new area.	A.M.
Etinehem	20/3/16		Moved to Montigny. in the afternoon went to the Dump at La Neuville near Corbie	A.M.
Montigny	21/3/16		Visited railhead + dump, chose another dump. as the first one was inconvenient. Visited dump again in afternoon	A.M.
Montigny	22/3/16		Visited dump in morning + again in the afternoon. Stores distributed to troops.	A.M.
Montigny	23/3/16		Visited dump both morning + afternoon no truck from Base	A.M.
Daours	24/3/16		Div. Head Qrs moved here this morning. Visited dump in afternoon distribution of Stores in progress	A.M.
Daours	25/3/16		Visited dump in morning.	A.M.
Daours	26/3/16		No truck from Base. Visited dump morning + afternoon	A.M.
Daours	27/3/16		Visited dump in morning. Amiens afternoon made local purchases for 30th Div School &c also Ailly sur Somme + found a dump + an office	A.M.
Daours	28/3/16		Moved to Ailly sur Somme. No truck from Base	A.M.

#353 Wt. W2544/1454 700,000 5/15 D. D. & L. A.D.S.S./Forms/C. 2118.

Instructions regarding War Diaries and Intelligence Summaries are contained in F. S. Regs., Part II. and the Staff Manual respectively. Title pages will be prepared in manuscript.

WAR DIARY
or
INTELLIGENCE SUMMARY.
(Erase heading not required.)

4th Sheet

Army Form C. 2118.

Place	Date	Hour	Summary of Events and Information	Remarks and references to Appendices
Ailly sur Somme	29/3/16		Stores arrived at Railhead (Still at Corbie) & distributed to troops as far as possible	APM
Ailly sur Somme	30/3/16		Stores distributed again to Troops. No truck from Base. arranged refilling at Etinehem for units in the 18th Div. Area	APM
Ailly sur Somme	31/3/16		Stores arrived from Railhead & distributed to troops. visited Amiens & purchased Stores urgently required by troops.	APM
			APM [signature] Lieutenant DADOS 30th Div. 31.3.16	APM

#353 Wt. W2544/1454 700,000 5/15 D. D. & L. A.D.S.S./Forms/C. 2118.

Instructions regarding War Diaries and Intelligence Summaries are contained in F. S. Regs., Part II. and the Staff Manual respectively. Title pages will be prepared in manuscript.

WAR DIARY
or
INTELLIGENCE SUMMARY.
(Erase heading not required.)

Army Form C. 2118.

DADOS 30 D Vol 6

Place	Date	Hour	Summary of Events and Information	Remarks and references to Appendices
			Confidential	
			War Diary of D.A.D.O.S. 30th Div.	
			From 1st April 1916 To. 30th April 1916	

2353 Wt. W2544/1454 700,000 5/15 D. D. & L. A.D.S.S./Forms/C. 2118.

Instructions regarding War Diaries and Intelligence Summaries are contained in F. S. Regs., Part II. and the Staff Manual respectively. Title pages will be prepared in manuscript.

WAR DIARY
or
INTELLIGENCE SUMMARY.
(Erase heading not required.)

1st Aut

Army Form C. 2118.

Place	Date	Hour	Summary of Events and Information	Remarks and references to Appendices
Ailly sur Somme	1/4/16		Published in Div. Routine orders the necessity of the submission of indents for Clothing & Equipment at short intervals, as cases have recently arisen where units after coming out of the trenches have indented for stores on a very large quantities, amounting in some instances to about 80% of whole strength. Four covers for Trench Helmets have been sent by O.O. XIII Corps Troops, thro' Q.M.G. for trial. vide 4th Army No. H.Q.A 4/1/4. XIII Corps No. Q.C. 264/217. — Stores arrived from Railhead & distributed to Troops. Refilled at Etinehem units of 89th Brigade & Arty units attached to 18th Divn.	AMR
Ailly sur Somme	2/4/16		Conference of D.M.S & Q.M.S's of division. 24 Lewis guns arrived from Base, bringing up establishment to 8 guns per Infy Batt. Stores distributed to units	AMR
Ailly sur Somme	3/4/16		Stores arrived from Base & distributed to troops. Visited Amiens in re [illegible] purchased stores urgently required	AMR
Ailly sur Somme	4/4/16		No truck from Base today. Visited R.O.O. to arrange about return of winter clothing &c &c to Base	AMR
Ailly s/Somme	5/4/16		P.H. Helmets arrived from Base, arranged distribution	AMR
Ailly s/Somme	6/4/16		Stores arrived from Base & distributed to troops.	
Ailly s/Somme	7/4/16		No truck from Base. Visited Corbie to find suitable store for storing winter clothing pending its return to Paris on 15th inst.	AMR

2353 Wt. W2544/1454 700,000 5/15 D. D. & L. A.D.S.S./Forms/C. 2118.

Instructions regarding War Diaries and Intelligence Summaries are contained in F. S. Regs., Part II. and the Staff Manual respectively. Title pages will be prepared in manuscript.

WAR DIARY
or
INTELLIGENCE SUMMARY.
(Erase heading not required.)

Army Form C. 2118.

2nd Sheet

Place	Date	Hour	Summary of Events and Information	Remarks and references to Appendices
Ailly s/Somme	8/4/16		Stores arrived from Base & distributed to troops	AMs
Ailly s/Somme	9/4/16		Board of Survey held on unserviceable clothing to be returned.	AMs
Ailly s/Somme	10/4/16		Stores arrived from Base & distributed to troops. Board of Survey held in Corbie district for the return of winter clothing &c	AMs
Ailly s/Somme	11/4/16		Stores arrived from Base & distributed to troops. Board of Survey at Argoeuves	AMs
Ailly s/Somme	12/4/16		No truck today.	
Ailly s/Somme	13/4/16		Stores arrived from Base & distributed to troops. Proceeded on leave to England for 10 days	AMs
Ailly s/Somme	19/4/16		Recalled from leave. Work in office & dump proceeding normally. Visited [illegible]	AMs
Ailly s/Somme	20/4/16		Stores arrived from Base & distributed to troops. Visited Railhead.	AMs
Ailly s/Somme	21/4/16		Stores arrived from Base & distributed to troops. Blankets returned to Base	AMs
Ailly s/Somme	22/4/16		No truck from Base. Arranged winter clothing to [illegible] to Base	AMs
Ailly s/Somme	23/4/16		Stores arrived at Railhead & distributed to troops. Handed over 2000 [illegible] Helmets to 7th Divn. Sent a truck of blankets to Base	AMs
Ailly s/Somme	24/4/16		No truck today from Base. Visited Railhead.	AMs
Ailly s/Somme	25/4/16		Stores arrived from Base & distributed to troops. Visited [illegible] & arranged for [illegible] [illegible] & Bags for carrying Mills grenades. [illegible]	AMs

2353 Wt. W2544/1454 700,000 5/15 D. D. & L. A.D.S.S./Forms/C. 2118.

Army Form C. 2118.

3rd Sheet

WAR DIARY
or
INTELLIGENCE SUMMARY.
(Erase heading not required.)

Instructions regarding War Diaries and Intelligence Summaries are contained in F. S. Regs., Part II. and the Staff Manual respectively. Title pages will be prepared in manuscript.

Place	Date	Hour	Summary of Events and Information	Remarks and references to Appendices
Ailly s/Somme	26/4/16		Purchased Service Colour paint as supplies cannot be obtained from Base. Stores arrived from Railhead + distributed to troops.	AMS.
Ailly s/Somme	27/4/16		Visited Railhead. Stores arrived from Base + were distributed to troops. another truck of winter-clothing re despatched to Base	AMS
Ailly s/Somme	28/4/16		No truck to day.	AMS.
Ailly s/Somme	29/4/16		Stores arrived from Base + distributed to troops. Truck of winter clothing despatched to Paris for disinfection. Lt F. Parker AOD arrived from 7th Division	AMS
Ailly s/Somme	30/4/16		Stores arrived from Base + distributed to troops. Visited Railhead. Truck of winter clothing despatched to Base: Collected Shell Jackets from Trench Mortar Batteries for the 2 additional pockets to be carried out locally, thus enabling them to carry 6 Stokes bombs instead of 4.	AMS.

A W Stewart Lieut
D.A.D.O.S.
30th Div

DADOS
30 DW
Vol 7

Army Form C. 2118.

Instructions regarding War Diaries and Intelligence Summaries are contained in F. S. Regs., Part II. and the Staff Manual respectively. Title pages will be prepared in manuscript.

WAR DIARY
or
INTELLIGENCE SUMMARY.
(Erase heading not required.)

Place	Date	Hour	Summary of Events and Information	Remarks and references to Appendices
			Confidential	
			War Diary	
			of	
			D.A.D.O.S., 30th Divn	
			From 1st May 1916 To 31st May 1916	

2353 Wt. W2544/1454 700,000 5/15 D. D. & L. A.D.S.S./Forms/C. 2118.

Army Form C. 2118.

WAR DIARY
or
INTELLIGENCE SUMMARY.

(Erase heading not required.)

Instructions regarding War Diaries and Intelligence Summaries are contained in F. S. Regs., Part II. and the Staff Manual respectively. Title pages will be prepared in manuscript.

1st Sheet

Place	Date	Hour	Summary of Events and Information	Remarks and references to Appendices
Ailly s/Somme	1/5/16		Stores arrived from Railhead & distributed to troops.	AMS
Ailly s/Somme	2/5/16		No truck today. Visited Amiens & carried out local purchase of stores urgently required by troops	AMS
Ailly s/Somme	3/5/16		Stores arrived from Railhead & distributed to troops. Visited Railhead which has been moved to HEILLY from today.	AMS.
Ailly s/Somme	4/5/16		No truck from Base today or tomorrow on account of the move.	AMS
Ailly s/Somme	5/5/16		Moved to Etinehem.	AMS
Etinehem	6/5/16		Stores arrived from Railhead & distributed to troops	AMS
Etinehem	7/5/16		" " " " " Visited Railhead.	F.P.
Etinehem	8/5/16		Attended Quartermasters meeting. Visited Amiens & carried out local purchase of stores urgently required – Visited R'hd.	F.P.
Etinehem	9/5/16		Visited ADOS & I.O.M. Part distribution of Steel Helmets	F.P.
Etinehem	10/5/16		Visited all Trench M. Batteries & collected steel helmets, also visited R'hd. and Amiens to make several local purchases of urgent stores. Called on ADOS & I.O.M.	F.P.
Etinehem	11/5/16		Stores arrived from R'hd & distributed to Troops.	F.P.
Etinehem	12/5/16		Visited Div! Company & 60. Army Troops. also Railhead.	F.P.

8353 Wt. W2544/1454 700,000 5/15 D. D. & L. A.D.S.S./Forms/C. 2118.

Instructions regarding War Diaries and Intelligence Summaries are contained in F. S. Regs., Part II. and the Staff Manual respectively. Title pages will be prepared in manuscript.

WAR DIARY
or
INTELLIGENCE SUMMARY.
(Erase heading not required.)

2nd Sheet.

Army Form C. 2118.

Place	Date	Hour	Summary of Events and Information	Remarks and references to Appendices
Etinehem	13/5/16		Visited Railhead + distributed stores to Troops. Collected [illegible] from Ordnance Corps Troops. + [illegible] from I.O.M.	[illegible]
Etinehem	14/5/16		ADOS [illegible] (evacuation) [illegible] Visited Railhead + distributed stores to Troops. Arranged with RDO [illegible]	[illegible]
Etinehem	15/5/16		Visited Amiens + made [illegible] purchase of stores urgently required by [illegible] Troops. [illegible] Corps Troops [illegible] Visited [illegible]	
Etinehem	16/5/16		Visited [illegible] + distributed stores to Troops. ADOS [illegible] I.O.M. to collect [illegible]	
Etinehem	17/5/16		Stores arrived from Railhead + distributed to Troops. Visited Railhead. Collected 4 Stromboss Horns from O.O. 4th Army Troops.	AMD
Etinehem	18/5/16		Stores arrived from Railhead + distributed to Troops. Lt. F. Parker A.O.D. left for duty with 18th Divn. Visited A.D.O.S.	AMD
Etinehem	19/5/16		Stores arrived from Railhead + distributed to Troops. Send Truck load of blankets to Railhead for despatch to Paris. Visited Railhead, Amiens for Local purchases + A.D.O.S.	AMD
Etinehem	20/5/16		Stores arrived from Railhead + distributed to Troops. Recd 7 Strombos Horns from O.O. XIII Corps.	AMD
Etinehem	21/5/16		Stores arrived from Railhead + distributed to Troops. Recd Shower Bath from O.O. XIII Corps Tps + issued it to 21st Infy Brigade	AMD
Etinehem	22/5/16		Stores arrived from Railhead + distributed to Troops. A.D.O.S. visited Store. Visited D.A.C. in afternoon	AMD
Etinehem	23/5/16		Stores arrived from Base + distributed to Troops. Visited A.D.O.S. in evening	AMD

2353 Wt. W2544/1454 700,000 5/15 D. D. & L. A.D.S.S./Forms/C. 2118.

Army Form C. 2118.

Instructions regarding War Diaries and Intelligence Summaries are contained in F. S. Regs., Part II. and the Staff Manual respectively. Title pages will be prepared in manuscript.

WAR DIARY
or
INTELLIGENCE SUMMARY.

(Erase heading not required.)

3rd Sheet

Place	Date	Hour	Summary of Events and Information	Remarks and references to Appendices
Etinehem	24/5/16		Stores arrived from Base & distributed to Troops.	AMS
Etinehem	25/5/16		Stores arrived from Base & distributed to Troops. Indented for 1560 canvas carriers & 780 Boxes for the carriers for the Hand carts for Lewis guns	AMS.
Etinehem	26/5/16		Visited Railhead. Stores arriving from Base distributed to Troops	AMS
Etinehem	27/5/16		Stores arrived from Railhead & issued to Troops	AMS
Etinehem	28/5/16		Stores arrived from Railhead & issued to Troops. Visited A.D.O.S.	AMS.
Etinehem	29/5/16		Stores arrived from Railhead & issued to Troops. Visited Amiens for local purchases	AMS
Etinehem	30/5/16		Stores arrived from Railhead & issued to Troops	AMS.
Etinehem	31/5/16		Visited Railhead & distributed stores received from Base to Troops	AMS.

A W Stewart [illegible]
DADOS
30/5/16 30 Div

2353 Wt. W2544/1454 700,000 5/15 D. D. & L. A.D.S.S. Forms/C. 2118.

DADOS 30th Div Vol 8 June

Army Form C. 2118.

Instructions regarding War Diaries and Intelligence Summaries are contained in F. S. Regs., Part II. and the Staff Manual respectively. Title pages will be prepared in manuscript.

WAR DIARY
or
INTELLIGENCE SUMMARY.
(Erase heading not required.)

Place	Date	Hour	Summary of Events and Information	Remarks and references to Appendices

Confidential

War Diary

of

DADOS. 30th Divn.

From 1st June 1916 To 30th June 1916.

2353 Wt. W2544/1454 700,000 5/15 D. D. & L. A.D.S.S. Forms/C. 2118.

Instructions regarding War Diaries and Intelligence Summaries are contained in F. S. Regs., Part II. and the Staff Manual respectively. Title pages will be prepared in manuscript.

WAR DIARY
or
INTELLIGENCE SUMMARY.
(Erase heading not required.)

Army Form C. 2118.

1st Sheet

Place	Date	Hour	Summary of Events and Information	Remarks and references to Appendices
Etinehem	1/6/16		Stores arrived from Railhead & have been distributed to Troops	AMD
Etinehem	2/6/16		Stores arrived from R'Head & distributed to Troops. Visited Amiens for urgent Local purchase	AMD
Etinehem	3/6/16		Stores arrived from R'Head – distributed to Troops. Attended A.D.O.S's office for conference	AMD
Etinehem	4/6/16		Stores arrived from Base have been distributed to Troops	AMD.
Etinehem	5/6/16		Stores arrived from Base have been distributed to Troops	AMD.
Etinehem	6/6/16		Stores arrived from Base, distributed to Troops.	AMD.
Etinehem	7/6/16		Attended conference of QM's & QMS's of the Divn. – Distributed Stores to Tps arriving from Base	AMD
Etinehem	8/6/16		A.D.O.S. visited the dump & found everything OK. Lewis Gun arrived for 20th L.F.C.	AMD.
Etinehem	9/6/16		Stores arrived from Railhead & distributed to Troops. Effected Local purchases in Amiens	AMD
Etinehem	10/6/16		Stores arrived from Railhead & Distributed to Troops.	AMD.
Etinehem	11/6/16		Wired to Base for 4.5 Q.F. complete with dial sight – to replace one destroyed by premature. D Batty 149 Bde	
			Stores arrived from Railhead distributed to Tps	AMD
Etinehem	12/6/16		Stores arrived from Railhead & distributed to Troops. ~~Gun for D/149 Bde arrived from Base~~	AMD.
Etinehem	13/6/16		Stores arrived from Railhead & distributed to Troops. Gun for D/149 Bde arrived from Base	AMD.
Etinehem	14/6/16		Stores arrived from Railhead & distributed Troops. Covers for working Parts of Lewis Guns arrived from Base also Tantalus bomb carriers from XIII Corps Troops.	AMD

2353 Wt. W2544/1454 700,000 5/15 D. D. & L. A.D.S.S. Forms/C. 2118.

Instructions regarding War Diaries and Intelligence Summaries are contained in F. S. Regs., Part II. and the Staff Manual respectively. Title pages will be prepared in manuscript.

WAR DIARY
or
INTELLIGENCE SUMMARY.
(Erase heading not required.)

2nd Sheet

Army Form C. 2118.

Place	Date	Hour	Summary of Events and Information	Remarks and references to Appendices
Eticchem	15/6/16		Stores arrived from Railhead & distributed to Troops. Visited Amiens on urgent local purchase. Tantalum Bomb Carriers issued to T.M. Btys.	AMS
Eticchem	16/6/16		Stores arrived from Railhead & distributed to Troops	AMS
Eticchem	17/6/16		Stores arrived from Railhead & distributed to Troops	AMS
Eticchem	18/6/16		Stores arrived from Railhead & distributed to Troops	AMS
Eticchem	19/6/16		Stores arrived from Railhead & distributed to Troops.	AMS
Eticchem	20/6/16		Stores arrived from Railhead & distributed to Troops. Visited Amiens for urgent local purchase of paint for camouflage of Tarpaulins	AMS
Eticchem	21/6/16		Stores arrived from Railhead & distributed to Troops	AMS
Eticchem	22/6/16		Stores arrived from Railhead & distributed to Troops	AMS
Eticchem	23/6/16		Stores arrived from Railhead & distributed to Troops. Visited Amiens for local purchase	AMS
Eticchem	24/6/16		Stores arrived from Railhead & distributed to Troops. 32 Hand Carts for Lewis Guns from Base	AMS
Eticchem	25/6/16		Stores arrived from Railhead & distributed to Troops. Further 40 Hand Carts for Lewis Guns arrived. Visited Amiens to bring out urgent Stores for Troops. A.D.O.S. called.	AMS
Eticchem	26/6/16		Stores arrived from Railhead & distributed to Troops	AMS

2353 Wt. W2544/1454 700,000 5/15 D. D. & L. A.D.S.S. Forms/C. 2118.

Army Form C. 2118.

Instructions regarding War Diaries and Intelligence Summaries are contained in F. S. Regs., Part II. and the Staff Manual respectively. Title pages will be prepared in manuscript.

WAR DIARY
or
INTELLIGENCE SUMMARY.
(Erase heading not required.)

3rd Sheet

Place	Date	Hour	Summary of Events and Information	Remarks and references to Appendices
Etinehem	27 6/16		Stores arrived from Railhead & distributed to Troops. A.D.O.S. visited dump.	[illegible]
Etinehem	28 6/16		Stores arrived from Railhead & distributed to Troops. Sent a Truck Load of Capes Macintosh to Base	[illegible]
Etinehem	29 6/16		Stores arrived from Base & distributed to Troops. A.D.O.S. visited dump. indented for Magazine Carriers for Lewis Guns on scale of 16 per gun.	[illegible]
Etinehem	30 6/16		Stores arrived from Base & distributed to Troops	[illegible]

[illegible signature]
D.A.D.O.S.
30th Divn.

30 July

Army Form C. 2118.

30 Div 2n DOS

Instructions regarding War Diaries and Intelligence Summaries are contained in F. S. Regs., Part II. and the Staff Manual respectively. Title pages will be prepared in manuscript.

WAR DIARY
or
INTELLIGENCE SUMMARY.

(Erase heading not required.)

Vol 9

Place	Date	Hour	Summary of Events and Information	Remarks and references to Appendices
			– Confidential – War Diary of DADOS 30th Div from July 1st 1916 to July 31st 1916	

2353 Wt. W2544/1454 700,000 5/15 D. D. & L. A.D.S.S. Forms/C. 2118.

Instructions regarding War Diaries and Intelligence Summaries are contained in F. S. Regs., Part II. and the Staff Manual respectively. Title pages will be prepared in manuscript.

WAR DIARY
or
INTELLIGENCE SUMMARY.
(*Erase heading not required.*)

1st Sheet

Army Form C. 2118.

Place	Date	Hour	Summary of Events and Information	Remarks and references to Appendices
Etinehem	1/7/16		Stores arrived from Base & distributed to Troops	AMS
Corbie	2/7/16		Moved from Etinehem, arranged for refilling Stores received from Base, at a point on Bray–Corbie road. K. 17 b 5.2	AMS
Corbie	3/7/16		Stores arrived at Refilling point from Base & were distributed to Troops. Visited refilling point. Divl H.Qrs & 90th Bde H.Qrs who are out of the line & require refitting.	AMS
Corbie	4/7/16		Stores arrived from Railhead & distributed to troops at refilling point.	AMS
Corbie	5/7/16		Stores arrived from Railhead & distributed to troops at refilling point. Attended conference at A.D.O.S's office. Attended conference of Q.Ms & A.M.S's at Div. H.Qrs on refitting. Visited dump & arranged to send Salvaged Stores to Base	AMS
Corbie	6/7/16		Stores arrived from Railhead & distributed to Troops. Visited Amiens for urgent local purchases in connection with refitting	AMS
Corbie	7/7/16		Stores arrived from Railhead & distributed to Troops. Despatched captured Stores to Base.	AMS
Corbie	8/7/16		Stores arrived from Railhead & distributed to Troops. Visited dump & Divl H.Qrs	AMS
Corbie	9/7/16		Despatched Captured & Salvaged Stores to Railhead. Visited dump & Divl H.Qrs	AMS

2353 Wt. W2544/1454 700,000 5/15 D. D. & L. A.D.S.S. Forms/C 2118.

Instructions regarding War Diaries and Intelligence Summaries are contained in F. S. Regs., Part II. and the Staff Manual respectively. Title pages will be prepared in manuscript.

WAR DIARY
or
INTELLIGENCE SUMMARY.
(Erase heading not required.)

2nd Sheet

Army Form C. 2118.

Place	Date	Hour	Summary of Events and Information	Remarks and references to Appendices
Corbie	10/7/16		Stores arrived from Railhead & distributed to Troops at advanced Refilling Point. Sent salved stores to Base & also captured German stores. Visited H.Q. at [illegible]	AMD
Corbie	11/7/16		Stores arrived from Railhead & distributed to Troops at advanced Refilling Point	AMD
Corbie	12/7/16		Stores arrived from Railhead & distributed to Troops at advanced Refilling Point. Visited Railhead. Dump & Div H.Qrs in afternoon.	AMD
Corbie	13/7/16		Stores arrived from Railhead & distributed to Troops at advanced Dump. D.A.Q.M.G. visited office. A.D.O.S. informed me of the probability of 11th Div being moved into 2nd Corps	AMD.
Corbie	14/7/16		Stores arrived from Railhead & distributed to Troops	AMD
Corbie	15/7/16		Further 72 Hand Carts for Lewis guns arrived from Base	AMD
Corbie	16/7/16		Stores arrived from Railhead & distributed to Troops	AMD
Corbie	17/7/16		Stores arrived from Railhead & distributed to Troops	AMD
Corbie	18/7/16		Stores arrived from Railhead & distributed to Troops	AMD
Corbie	19/7/16		Stores arrived from Railhead & distributed to Troops.	AMD
Corbie	20/7/16		H.Qrs move to CITADEL. This office remains here. Stores distributed to Troops	AMD
Corbie	21/7/16		Stores arrived from Railhead & distributed to Troops. Visited D.O.M. & [illegible] Workshops	AMD

2353 Wt. W2544/1454 700,000 5/15 D. D. & L. A.D.S.S./Forms/C. 2118.

Instructions regarding War Diaries and Intelligence Summaries are contained in F. S. Regs., Part II. and the Staff Manual respectively. Title pages will be prepared in manuscript.

WAR DIARY
or
INTELLIGENCE SUMMARY.
(*Erase heading not required.*)

3rd Sheet –

Army Form C. 2118.

Place	Date	Hour	Summary of Events and Information	Remarks and references to Appendices
Corbie	22/7/16		Visited Divl H.Qrs at Billon Copse. Arranged to move Office up to advanced Dump on Bray Albert Road. Stores arrived from Base & Units refilled as far as possible	AMS
F.19.D.	23/7/16		Moved to advance Dump. Stores arrived at new Railhead "Edgehill" & distributed to Troops. Visited 'G' & 'Q' offices. AA & QMG visited dump.	AMS
F.19.D.	24/7/16		Stores distributed to Troops. DAQMG visited dump	AMS
F.19.D	25/7/16		No truck today. Sent to H.M. W'shops for spare parts for 2" T. Mortars	AMS
F.19.D	26/7/16		Stores arrived from Railhead & distributed to Troops. ADOS visited dump. Visited D.H.Q. at Battle dug-out.	AMS
F.19.D	27/7/16		Stores arrived from Railhead & distributed to Troops. Visited R.Head & DOM.	AMS.
F.19.D	28/7/16		Stores arrived from Railhead & distributed to Troops. ADOS visited dump	AMS
F.19.D	29/7/16		Stores arrived from Railhead & distributed to Troops	AMS
F.19.D	30/7/16		Stores arrived from Railhead & distributed to Troops	AMS
F.19.D	31/7/16		ADOS visited dump. Stores issued to Troops.	AMS.

2353 Wt. W2544/1454 700,000 5/15 D. D. & L. A.D.S.S. Forms/C. 2118.

Instructions regarding War Diaries and Intelligence Summaries are contained in F. S. Regs., Part II. and the Staff Manual respectively. Title pages will be prepared in manuscript.

WAR DIARY
or
INTELLIGENCE SUMMARY.
(Erase heading not required.)

Army Form C. 2118.

DADOS
VOL 10

Place	Date	Hour	Summary of Events and Information	Remarks and references to Appendices
			– Confidential –	
			War Diary	
			of	
			DADOS	
			30th Divn	
			From August 1st 1916 To Aug 31st 1916	

2353 Wt. W2544/1454 700,000 5/15 D. D. & L. A.D.S.S. Forms/C. 2118.

Instructions regarding War Diaries and Intelligence Summaries are contained in F. S. Regs., Part II. and the Staff Manual respectively. Title pages will be prepared in manuscript.

WAR DIARY
or
INTELLIGENCE SUMMARY.
(Erase heading not required.)

Army Form C. 2118.

1st Sheet

Place	Date	Hour	Summary of Events and Information	Remarks and references to Appendices
F.19.D	1 8/16		Stores arrived from Railhead & distributed to troops. arranged to move to Hangest.	AMO
F.19.D	2 8/16		moved to Hangest. reconsigned all stores to XI Corps Railhead	AMO
HANGEST	3 8/16		Transferred to X Corps. ADOS called. arranged removal of stores on to Trucks	AMO
Hangest	4 8/16		Transferred to XI Corps 1st Army. Removed all stores from dump to R'Head	AMO
Hangest	5 8/16		moved to Bethune, visited HQ at Busnes. ADOS at Hinges.	AMO
Bethune	6 8/16		A.D.O.S. called, visited Railhead. arranged for store & offices	AMO
Bethune	7 8/16		Seven trucks of stores + 2 two open trucks containing vehicles at Railhead. Enemy shelling this town.	AMO
Bethune	8 8/16		One P.H.G. Helmet per Officer & O.R. arrived from Base to replace one P.H. Visited Railhead & Div H.Q.	AMO
Bethune	9 8/16		Stores arrived from Base & distributed to Troops. ADOS called.	AMO
Bethune	10 8/16		Stores arrived from Base & distributed to Troops.	AMO
Bethune	11 8/16		D.D.O.S. 1st Army visited dump & office. Stores arrived from Base issued to Troops	AMO
Bethune	12 8/16		Divl HQrs moved from Busnes to Bethune. Stores arriving from Base being issued to Tps	AMO
Bethune	13 8/16		Stores arrived from Base & distributed to Troops. ADOS visited Dump	AMO
Bethune	14 8/16		Stores arrived from Base & distributed to Troops. Visited D.A.M.	AMO

Instructions regarding War Diaries and Intelligence Summaries are contained in F. S. Regs., Part II. and the Staff Manual respectively. Title pages will be prepared in manuscript.

WAR DIARY
or
INTELLIGENCE SUMMARY.
(Erase heading not required.)

2nd Sheet

Army Form C. 2118.

Place	Date	Hour	Summary of Events and Information	Remarks and references to Appendices
Bethune	15/8/16		Stores received from Railhead have been issued to Troops. A.D.O.S. visited store	A.M.S.
Bethune	16/8/16		Formation of Armourers Shop. 2 Armourers from each Inf. Bde detailed	A.M.S.
Bethune	17/8/16		Lieut Evetts reported for duty in formation of Armourers Shop. Stores arrived from Base & distributed to Troops	A.M.S.
Bethune	18/8/16		Stores arrived from Base & issued to Troops. A.D.O.S. visited Office Store & Shops.	A.M.S.
Bethune	19/8/16		Stores arrived from Railhead & distributed to Troops. A.D.O.S. visited office in afternoon	A.M.S.
Bethune	20/8/16		Stores arrived from Railhead distributed to Troops. Visited Railhead	A.M.S.
Bethune	21/8/16		Stores arrived from Railhead & distributed to Troops. Visited Armourers Shop & other shops. A.D.O.S. called in afternoon	A.M.S.
Bethune	22/8/16		Stores received from Base & issued to Troops. Visited Railhead [illegible]	A.M.S.
Bethune	23/8/16		Stores arrived from Base & issued to Troops. A.D.O.S. [illegible] visited D.O.M.	A.M.S.
	24/8/16		Stores arrived from Railhead distributed to Troops. Visited Railhead	A.M.S.
	25/8/16		Stores arrived from Railhead distributed to Troops. A.D.O.S. called	A.M.S.
	26/8/16		Went to Hazebrouck to purchase White lead. Called [illegible]	A.M.S.
	27/8/16		Lt Evetts left to join IV Corps. Stores arrived from Base & distributed to Troops. [illegible]	A.M.S.

2353 Wt. W2544/1454 700,000 5/15 D. D. & L. A.D.S.S. Forms/C. 2118.

Army Form C. 2118.

WAR DIARY
or
INTELLIGENCE SUMMARY.
(Erase heading not required.)

3rd Sheet.

Instructions regarding War Diaries and Intelligence Summaries are contained in F. S. Regs., Part II. and the Staff Manual respectively. Title pages will be prepared in manuscript.

Place	Date	Hour	Summary of Events and Information	Remarks and references to Appendices
Bethune	28/8/16.		Stores received from Base & issued to Troops. Visited railhead	AMS
Bethune	29/8/16		Stores received from Base & issued to Troops. Visited Infy School & Anti gas School ADOS called. Sent 4 3" Mortars to 1st Army T M School & 1 to Div TM School.	AMS
Bethune	30/8/16		Stores arrived from Railhead & distributed to Troops. Visited Shops & OO XI C Tps	AMS
Bethune	31/8/16		Stores arrived from Railhead & issued to Troops. visited Railhead.	AMS

2353 Wt. W2544/1454 700,000 5/15 D. D. & L. A.D.S.S. Forms/C 2118.

Instructions regarding War Diaries and Intelligence Summaries are contained in F. S. Regs., Part II. and the Staff Manual respectively. Title pages will be prepared in manuscript.

WAR DIARY
or
INTELLIGENCE SUMMARY.
(Erase heading not required.)

Army Form C. 2118.

Vol 11

Place	Date	Hour	Summary of Events and Information	Remarks and references to Appendices
			— Confidential —	
			War Diary	
			of	
			D A D O S	
			30th Div	
			from Sept 1st 1916 to Sept ~~1st~~ 30th/16	

2353 Wt. W2544/1454 700,000 5/15 D. D. & L. A.D.S.S. Forms/C. 2118.

Instructions regarding War Diaries and Intelligence Summaries are contained in F. S. Regs., Part II. and the Staff Manual respectively. Title pages will be prepared in manuscript.

WAR DIARY
or
INTELLIGENCE SUMMARY.
(Erase heading not required.)

1st Sheet

Army Form C. 2118.

Place	Date	Hour	Summary of Events and Information	Remarks and references to Appendices
Bethune	1 9/16		Stores arrived at Railhead, cleared & distributed to Troops. Visited Railhead	AM
"	2 9/16		Stores arrived from Railhead & distributed to Troops. ADOS called.	AM
"	3 9/16		Stores received from Calais issued to Troops. Visited D.O.M. & Railhead. ADOS called	AM
"	4 9/16		Stores arrived from Railhead & distributed to Troops. Visited A.M. Workshops.	AM
"	5 9/16		Stores arrived from Railhead & distributed to Troops. Visited ADOS. Visited Salvage Dump	AM
"	6 9/16		Stores arrived from Railhead & distributed to Troops. 1 Blanket per man being issued	AM
"	7 9/16		Stores received from Base & distributed to Troops. 4000 Gum Boots allotted to Divn. ADOS called	AM
"	8 9/16		Stores received from Base & distributed to Troops. Visited Railhead	AM
"	9 9/16		Stores received from Base & distributed to Troops. ADOS called.	AM
"	10 9/16		Stores received from Base & distributed to Troops. Visited DOM. Visited Salvage Dumps	AM
"	11 9/16		Stores arrived from Railhead - distributed to Troops. ADOS visited dump & office & Shops.	AM
"	12 9/16		Stores arrived from Railhead & distributed to Troops. Visited Railhead	AM
"	13 9/16		Stores arrived from Railhead & distributed to Troops. Old Clothing receipt store to be kept	AM
"	14 9/16		Stores arrived from Base & distributed to Troops. ADOS visited office & Dump.	AM
"	15 9/16		Stores received from Railhead issued to Troops. Visited Infy School & Railhead	AM
"	16 9/16		Stores received from Base issued to Troops. ADOS called	AM

2353 Wt. W2544/1454 700,000 5/15 D. D. & L. A.D.S.S. Forms/C. 2118.

Instructions regarding War Diaries and Intelligence Summaries are contained in F. S. Regs., Part II. and the Staff Manual respectively. Title pages will be prepared in manuscript.

WAR DIARY
or
INTELLIGENCE SUMMARY.
(Erase heading not required.)

2nd Sheet

Army Form C. 2118.

Place	Date	Hour	Summary of Events and Information	Remarks and references to Appendices
Bethune	17 9/16		Havre Base will supply stores from today inclusive. Stores received from Base & issued to troops	AMS
"	18 9/16		Arrangements being made to send all ordnance stores from this dump to 4th Army area. Stores received from Railhead. ADOS. called. Transferred from [illegible] to XIII Corps Reserve Army	AMS
"	19 9/16		Entrain at 7 a.m. for Doullens. No truck from Base. Arrived at Doullens	AMS
Doullens	20 9/16		No truck from Base. Visited Vignacourt to find Office & Dump.	AMS
Doullens	21 9/16		Proceeded to Vignacourt. No truck from Base. Transferred to X Corps IV Army	AMS
Vignacourt	22 9/16		No truck from Base. ADOS X Corps visited office. Visited Railhead	AMS
"	23 9/16		Stores received from Base & distributed to Troops. Visited railhead	AMS
"	24 9/16		Stores received from Base. ADOS called at office. Visited railhead	AMS
"	25 9/16		No truck today. Visited railhead	AMS
"	26 9/16		Visited ADOS at Long. Arty joined XV Corps.	AMS
"	27 9/16		Lorries to Traffic 1st & 4th Army to Base trucks. Stores received from Base	AMS
"	28 9/16		Stores despatched from Bethune on 19th inst. only arrived today. No truck from Base	AMS
"	29 9/16		Stores arrived from Base & distributed to Troops.	AMS
"	30 9/16		Refilled Artillery, Pioneers &c. at advanced Refilling Point on Bray - Albert Road, distributed stores to other units in this area.	AMS.

2353 Wt. W2544/1454 700,000 5/15 D. D. & L. A.D.S.S. Forms/C. 2118.

Army Form C. 2118.

Vol 12

Instructions regarding War Diaries and Intelligence Summaries are contained in F. S. Regs., Part II. and the Staff Manual respectively. Title pages will be prepared in manuscript.

WAR DIARY
or
INTELLIGENCE SUMMARY.
(Erase heading not required.)

Place	Date	Hour	Summary of Events and Information	Remarks and references to Appendices
			Confidential War Diary of D.A.D.O.S. 50th Divn. from 18th October 1916 to October 31st 1916.	

*353 Wt. W2544/1454 700,000 5/15 D. D. & L. A.D.S.S./Forms/C. 2118.

Instructions regarding War Diaries and Intelligence Summaries are contained in F. S. Regs., Part II. and the Staff Manual respectively. Title pages will be prepared in manuscript.

WAR DIARY
or
INTELLIGENCE SUMMARY.
(*Erase heading not required.*)

1st Sheet

Army Form C. 2118.

Place	Date	Hour	Summary of Events and Information	Remarks and references to Appendices
Viguacourt	1/10/16		Stores arrived from Base & distributed to Troops. Blankets starting to arrive.	AMB
"	2/10/16		Stores arrived from Base & distributed to Troops. Visited Railhead. ADOS called	AMB
"	3/10/16		Stores arrived from Base & reconsigned to new Railhead. Visited new area	AMB
Ribemont	4/10/16		Moved to Ribemont. XV Corps. Visited Railhead. New C Clerk (Drake) arrived	AMB
"	5/10/16		Stores arrived from Base & distributed to Troops. ADOS XV Corps called. Visited R'head	AMB
"	6/10/16		a/S/Cdr C A Baader left for Havre on taking up commission in A.O.D. Stores distributed	AMB
"	7/10/16		Stores received from Base distributed to Troops. 26 Lewis Guns received for augmentation to 10 guns per Batt'n. Visited ADOS	AMB
"	8/10/16		Stores received from Base & distributed to Troops. Visited Railhead	AMB
"	9/10/16		Stores received from Base & distributed to Troops.	AMB
"	10/10/16		Stores received from Base & refilled units at Becordel. Visited ADOS. Visited D.O.M.'s	AMB
"	11/10/16		Stores arrived from Base & refilled units. Visited Railhead & H.M. Workshops	AMB
"	12/10/16		Stores arrived from Base & distributed to Troops. Went to Bellevue Farm & found a dump	AMB
"	13/10/16		Railhead changes from Méricourt to Edgehill Siding. Moved to vicinity of Bellevue Farm. & refilled units as before. E.10.D.1.1.	AMB
"	14/10/16		Stores arrived from Base & distributed to Troops	AMB
E.10.D.1.1				

2353 Wt. W2544/1454 700,000 5/15 D. D. & L. A.D.S.S./Forms/C 2118.

Instructions regarding War Diaries and Intelligence Summaries are contained in F. S. Regs., Part II. and the Staff Manual respectively. Title pages will be prepared in manuscript.

WAR DIARY
or
INTELLIGENCE SUMMARY.
(*Erase heading not required.*)

2nd Sheet

Army Form C. 2118.

Place	Date	Hour	Summary of Events and Information	Remarks and references to Appendices
E.10.D.1.1	15 10/16		D.A.Q.M.G. Called. Visited Railhead. Stores received from Base distributed to Troops	AMS
E.10.D.1.1	16 10/16		Stores received from Base distributed to Troops. Visited Amiens for urgent local purchase.	AMS
E.10.D.1.1	17 10/16		Stores received from Base distributed to Troops including 25% F.S. Dots. Visited H.M.W. shops at [illegible]	AMS
do	18 10/16		Stores arrived from Railhead & distributed to Troops. Visited Railhead including [illegible]	AMS
do	19 10/16		Stores arrived from Railhead & distributed to Troops. Including Horse Rugs.	AMS
do	20 10/16		Stores arrived from Base & issued to Troops. Visited ADOS & DOM.	AMS
do	21 10/16		Stores arrived from Base & distributed to Troops. Visited Railhead	AMS
do	22 10/16		Stores arrived from Base & distributed to Troops. 2 men from Anti Gas School reported for duty.	AMS
do	23 10/16		Stores arrived from Base & distributed to Troops. Visited ADOS	AMS
do	24 10/16		Stores arrived from Base & distributed to Troops.	AMS
do	25 10/16		Stores arrived from Base distributed to Troops. Cancelled trucks for 2 or 3 days	AMS
do	26 10/16		No truck, moved to BOUQUEMAISON. No stores or billets available till morning	AMS
Bouquemaison	27 10/16		No truck. formed office Store & billets. informed Q. [illegible] Corps	AMS
Bouquemaison	28 10/16		No truck today. Visited ADOS VII Corps & went to BAVINCOURT to see prospective dump.	AMS
do	29 10/16		No truck today. Visited Railhead & ADOS. Visited DADOS. 46th Div. Ref. [illegible]	AMS
do	30 10/16		No truck today. advised Corps prepare to receive stores at new Railhead WARLINCOURT	AMS
do	31 10/16		Proceeded to BAVINCOURT. Stores arriving from Corps dump also from Base & being distributed to Troops. Railhead SAULTY-LARBRET	AMS

2353 Wt. W2544/1454 700,000 5/15 D. D. & L. A.D.S.S./Forms/C. 2118.

Instructions regarding War Diaries and Intelligence Summaries are contained in F. S. Regs., Part II. and the Staff Manual respectively. Title pages will be prepared in manuscript.

WAR DIARY
or
INTELLIGENCE SUMMARY.
(Erase heading not required.)

Army Form C. 2118.

Vol 13

Place	Date	Hour	Summary of Events and Information	Remarks and references to Appendices
			War Diary of D.A.D.O.S. 30th Div. From Nov 1st 1916 to Nov 30th 1916.	

2353 Wt. W2544/1454 700,000 5/15 D. D. & L. A.D.S.S./Forms/C 2118.

Army Form C. 2118.

WAR DIARY
or
INTELLIGENCE SUMMARY.
(Erase heading not required.)

1st Sheet

Instructions regarding War Diaries and Intelligence Summaries are contained in F. S. Regs., Part II. and the Staff Manual respectively. Title pages will be prepared in manuscript.

Place	Date	Hour	Summary of Events and Information	Remarks and references to Appendices
Barincourt	1/11/16		Stores arrived from Base & distributed to Troops. D.D.O.S. Third Army called.	AHM
do	2/11/16		Stores arrived from Base & distributed to Troops. Visited Railhead.	AHM
do	3/11/16		Stores arrived from Base & distributed to Troops. ADOS called	AHM
do	4/11/16		Stores arrived from Base & distributed to Troops. Visited H.M. W'shops FREVENT	AHM
do	5/11/16		Stores arrived at Railhead & distributed to Troops. Visited Rl Head. ADOS called	AHM
do	6/11/16		Stores arrived at Railhead & issued to Troops.	AHM
do	7/11/16		Stores arrived from Base & distributed to Troops. A.D.O.S called	AHM
do	8/11/16		Stores arrived at Railhead & issued to Troops. Visited I.O.M.	AHM
do	9/11/16		Stores arrived from Base & distributed to Troops. Visited Railhead	AHM
do	10/11/16		Stores arrived from Base & distributed to Troops. ADOS called	AHM
do	11/11/16		Stores arrived from Base & issued to Troops. DDOS & ADOS called	AHM
do	12/11/16		Stores received from Base & distributed to Troops.	AHM
do	13/11/16		Stores received from Base & distributed to Troops. Visited H M W'shops	AHM
do	14/11/16		Stores received from Base & issued to Troops. ADOS called & inspected dump	AHM
do	15/11/16		Stores received from Railhead & distributed to Troops. Visited railhead	AHM
do	16		Stores received from Base & issued to Troops. A.D.O.S visited office & shops	AHM
do	17		Stores received from Base & distributed to Troops.	AHM
do	18		Stores received from Base & distributed to Troops.	AHM
do.	19		Stores arrived from Railhead & issued to Troops. Lt A H Williams joined for instruction	AHM

2353 Wt. W2544/1454 700,000 5/15 D. D. & L. A.D.S.S./Forms/C. 2118.

Instructions regarding War Diaries and Intelligence Summaries are contained in F. S. Regs., Part II. and the Staff Manual respectively. Title pages will be prepared in manuscript.

WAR DIARY
or
INTELLIGENCE SUMMARY.

(Erase heading not required.)

2nd Sheet

Army Form C. 2118.

Place	Date	Hour	Summary of Events and Information	Remarks and references to Appendices
BAVINCOURT	20/11/16		Stores received from Base distributed to Troops. [illegible] Capt for 14th Div	AM
do	21/11/16		Stores received from Railhead & issued to Troops. ADOS visited office [illegible]	AM
do	22/11/16		Stores received from Base & distributed to Troops. ADOS called	AM
do	23/11/16		Stores received from Base & issued to Troops. ADOS called	AM
do	24/11/16		Stores received from Base & issued to Troops. Visited Railhead	AM
do	25/11/16		Stores received from Base & issued to Troops. ADOS called.	AM
do	26/11/16		Stores received from Base & issued to Troops	AM
do	27/11/16		Stores received from Base & issued to Troops. Visited [illegible] Workshops.	AM
do	28/11/16		Stores received from Base & issued to Troops. Visited Railhead & [illegible]	AM
do	29/11/16		Stores received from Railhead & distributed to Troops	AM
do	30/11/16		Stores received from Railhead & distributed to Troops. Conference at Corps HQ.	AM

2353 Wt. W2544/1454 700,000 5/15 D. D. & L. A.D.S.S./Forms/C. 2118.

Instructions regarding War Diaries and Intelligence Summaries are contained in F. S. Regs., Part II. and the Staff Manual respectively. Title pages will be prepared in manuscript.

WAR DIARY
or
INTELLIGENCE SUMMARY.
(Erase heading not required.)

Army Form C. 2118.

Vol 14

Place	Date	Hour	Summary of Events and Information	Remarks and references to Appendices
			War Diary of D.A.D.O.S. 30th Divn from Dec 1st 1916 to Dec 31st 1916.	

Instructions regarding War Diaries and Intelligence Summaries are contained in F. S. Regs., Part II. and the Staff Manual respectively. Title pages will be prepared in manuscript.

WAR DIARY
or
INTELLIGENCE SUMMARY.
(Erase heading not required.)

R. E. Shiel

Army Form C. 2118.

Place	Date	Hour	Summary of Events and Information	Remarks and references to Appendices
Bavincourt	1/12/16		Stores arrived from Base & distributed to Troops. ADOS visited office & dump	AM
"	2/12/16		Do. Do. Visited Railhead	AM
"	3/12/16		Do. Do. Visited DOM ADOS visited me	AM
"	4/12/16		Do. Do. DDOS III Army & ADOS visited & inspected	AM
"	5/12/16		Do. Do. Visited Railhead & Inf. School	AM
"	6/12/16		Do. Do. ADOS visited dump & shops	AM
"	7/12/16		Do. Do. ADOS visited office	AM
"	8/12/16		Do. Do. GOC inspected dump & shops	AM
"	9/12/16		Do. Do. DAQMG inspected dump & shops.	AM
"	10		Do. Do. DADOS [illegible]	AM
"	11		Do. Do. ADOS visited office	AM
"	12		Do. Do. Lieut Williams left to take up duties as DADOS 49 Div	AM
"	13		Do. Do. ADOS called	AM
"	14		Do. Do.	AM
"	15		Do. Do. ADOS called	AM
"	16		Do. Do. " "	AM

2353 Wt. W2534/1454 700,000 5/15 D. D. & L. A.D.S.S./Forms/C. 2118.

Army Form C. 2118.

Instructions regarding War Diaries and Intelligence Summaries are contained in F. S. Regs., Part II. and the Staff Manual respectively. Title pages will be prepared in manuscript.

WAR DIARY
or
INTELLIGENCE SUMMARY.
(Erase heading not required.)

2nd Sheet

Place	Date	Hour	Summary of Events and Information	Remarks and references to Appendices
Bavincourt	17/12/16		Stores arrived from Base + distributed to Troops. ADOS visited dump	AM
"	18		Do Do {Establishment of Lewis guns increased from 10 to 12 per Battn.	AM
"	19		Do Do [+ demanded from Base. ADOS called	AM
"	20.		Do Do A.D.O.S. called	AM
"	21		Do Do D.A.D.O.S. returned from leave	AM
"	22		Do Do Visited Railhead. I O M + Laundry	AM
"	23		Do Do A.D.O.S. visited office + dump.	AM
"	24		Do Do.	AM
"	25		Do Do	AM
"	26		Do Do. Cond. Drake replaced by A/Sgt E. J. Perrin as chief clerk	AM
"	27		Do Do. A.D.O.S. visited dump + Shops. Visited Railhead	AM
"	28		Do Do. D.D.O.S. III Army + A.D.O.S. visited dump Shops + office	AM
"	29		Do Do	AM
"	30		Do Do. A.D.O.S. visited office.	AM
"	31		Do Do. Proceeded to Amiens on urgent local purchase for a raid.	AM

2353 Wt. W2544/1454 700,000 5/15 D. D. & L. A.D.S.S. Forms/C. 2118.

Instructions regarding War Diaries and Intelligence Summaries are contained in F. S. Regs., Part II. and the Staff Manual respectively. Title pages will be prepared in manuscript.

WAR DIARY
or
INTELLIGENCE SUMMARY.
(Erase heading not required.)

Army Form C. 2118.

Vol 15

Place	Date	Hour	Summary of Events and Information	Remarks and references to Appendices
			WAR DIARY of DADOS 30th Divn. From 1st January 1917 to 31st January 1917	

2353 Wt. W2544/1454 700,000 5/15 D. D. & L. A.D.S.S. Forms/C. 2118.

Instructions regarding War Diaries and Intelligence Summaries are contained in F. S. Regs., Part II. and the Staff Manual respectively. Title pages will be prepared in manuscript.

WAR DIARY
or
INTELLIGENCE SUMMARY.
(Erase heading not required.)

1st Sheet

Army Form C. 2118.

Place	Date	Hour	Summary of Events and Information	Remarks and references to Appendices
BAVINCOURT	Jan. 1st 1917		New traffic arrangements having been made. Trucks of Ordnance Stores will be sent to formations on alternate days instead of every day. Truck of stores arrived at Railhead, collected & distributed to troops. Visited Railhead & I.O.M. DADOS 49th Div came about taking over	AMD.
"	2/1/17		Visited DADOS 49th Div. saw office dump & shops at Lucheux	AMD
"	3/1/17		Stores received from Base & distributed to Troops. ADOS visited office & dump.	AMD
"	4/1/17		Lewis Gun Hand-carts to be abolished. This division having had authority to retain limbered wagons on previous re-organisation of Artillery, are complete. Battalions (Infy) instructed to return Hand-carts to store.	AMD
"	5/1/17		Attended conference at VII Corps H.Qrs. DDOS visited office, dump & shops in afternoon	AMD
"	6/1/17		Moved to Lucheux. VII Corps wired auth. to return Lewis Gun Hand-carts to Base	AMD.
Lucheux	7/1/17		Truck of Stores arrived at Railhead, cleared & distributed to Troops. ADOS. called	AMD
"	8/1/17		Truck received at Railhead & Stores issued to Tps. Lt Sir E M Nightingale Bt. reported for duty	AMD
"	9/1/17		Visited Amiens & carried out local purchases for Troops.	AMD
"	10/1/17		Stores received from Base & distributed to Troops. Visited I.O.M. & Railhead	AMD
"	11/1/17		Conference of Town Majors in the area. Truck from Base & Stores distributed to Troops	AMD
"	12/1/17		Stores received from railhead & issued to Troops. Visited Town Major Mondicourt with reference to Tentage for MHOW Pioneers	AMD

2353 Wt. W2544/1454 700,000 5/15 D. D. & L. A.D.S.S. Forms/C. 2118.

Instructions regarding War Diaries and Intelligence Summaries are contained in F. S. Regs., Part II. and the Staff Manual respectively. Title pages will be prepared in manuscript.

WAR DIARY
or
INTELLIGENCE SUMMARY.
(Erase heading not required.)

2nd Sheet

Army Form C. 2118.

Place	Date	Hour	Summary of Events and Information	Remarks and references to Appendices
Lucheux	13/7/17		Visited A.D.O.S. at VII Corps H.Qrs. also O.O. VII Corps Tps regarding stores for Indian pioneers	A.M.
"	14/7/17		D.D.O.S. III Army inspected Shops, dump & office.	A.M.
"	15/7/17		Proceeded to Amiens for urgent Local Purchase. Stores received from base & issued to Troops	A.M.
"	16/7/17		Visited Railhead. collected Electric arming rests from VII Corps for issue to Artillery	A.M.
"	17/7/17		Stores arrived from Base & distributed to Troops. The Base are making Covers for Steel Helmets	A.M.
"	18/7/17		Visited Amiens to collect stores purchased locally.	A.M.
"	19/7/17		Visited Indian Pioneers with D.A.Q.M.G. Stores arrived from Base & distributed to Troops	A.M.
"	20/7/17		Stores received from Base & distributed to Troops	A.M.
"	21/7/17		30th Supply Column joined the Division in place of 21st who rejoined 21st Divn	A.M.
"	22/7/17		Attended conference of Staff Captains. Quartermasters & O.M.S.s of the Division	A.M.
"	23/7/17		Stores arrived at Railhead from Base & issued to Troops. A.D.O.S. visited office dump & shops	A.M.
"	24/7/17		4th Blanket per man authorised by Corps for issue to Pioneers (Indian) Visited D.O.M.	A.M.
"	25/7/17		Stores arrived at Railhead & distributed to Troops	A.M.
"	26/7/17		A.D.O.S. called in the morning. Visited Amiens in afternoon & purchased urgent stores	A.M.
"	27/7/17		Stores arrived from Base. issued to units in the Divn Visited Railhead	A.M.
"	28/7/17		Visited Doullens & Amiens obtained Stores urgently required by troops	A.M.

2353 Wt. W2544/1454 700,000 5/15 D. D. & L. A.D.S.S. Forms/C. 2118.

Instructions regarding War Diaries and Intelligence Summaries are contained in F. S. Regs., Part II. and the Staff Manual respectively. Title pages will be prepared in manuscript.

WAR DIARY
or
INTELLIGENCE SUMMARY.
(Erase heading not required.)

3rd Sheet

Army Form C. 2118.

Place	Date	Hour	Summary of Events and Information	Remarks and references to Appendices
Lucheux	29/1/17		Stores arrived from Base & were distributed to Troops. Trouble with lorries owing to frost.	AM
"	30/1/17		A.D.O.S. called & inspected books & incidents of 89th Bde. Visited R.A. H.Q.	AM
"	31/1/17		Stores arrived from Base & were issued to Troops. Visited D.A.D.O.S. 14th Divn & arranged details regarding our Arty taking over 14th Divn guns.	AM

A. M. [illegible] Capt
D.A.D.O.S.
30 Divn
31/1/17

2353 Wt. W2544/1454 700,000 5/15 D. D. & L. A.D.S.S. Forms/C. 2118.

Instructions regarding War Diaries and Intelligence Summaries are contained in F. S. Regs., Part II. and the Staff Manual respectively. Title pages will be prepared in manuscript.

WAR DIARY
or
INTELLIGENCE SUMMARY.
(Erase heading not required.)

Army Form C. 2118.

Vol 16

Place	Date	Hour	Summary of Events and Information	Remarks and references to Appendices
			Confidential War Diary of D.A.D.O.S. 30th Divn from Feby 1st 1917 to Feby 28th 1917	

2353 Wt. W2544/1454 700,000 5/15 D. D. & L. A.D.S.S. Forms/C. 2118.

Instructions regarding War Diaries and Intelligence Summaries are contained in F. S. Regs., Part II. and the Staff Manual respectively. Title pages will be prepared in manuscript.

WAR DIARY
or
INTELLIGENCE SUMMARY.
(Erase heading not required.)

1st Sheet

Army Form C. 2118.

Place	Date	Hour	Summary of Events and Information	Remarks and references to Appendices
Lucheux	1 2/17		Attended conference at Corps H.Qrs. Lieut Sir Em Nightingale Bt AOD left for OQA Train	a/m
"	2 2/17		Truck of stores arrived at Railhead, collected, + distributed to Troops	a/m.
"	3 2/17		ADOS visited office dump + shops. visited railhead afterwards carried out urgent local purchase.	a/m
"	4 2/17		Railhead changed from BOUQUEMAISON to SAULTY-LARBRET.	a/m
"	5 2/17		Office moved to BERNEVILLE. Truck of stores at Railhead, collected + taken to new dump.	a/m
BERNEVILLE	6 2/17		Stores moved to BERNEVILLE. very bad accomodation for stores. original dump chosen having been bunked	a/m
"	7 2/17		ADOS visited dump + office. arranged with Town Major to have Nissen huts erected for stores.	a/m
"	8 2/17		Remainder of stores removed from LUCHEUX to BERNEVILLE.	a/m
"	9 2/17		Stores arrived at Railhead + distributed to Troops.	a/m
"	10 2/17		Visited Salvage Officer. Truck of stores arrived at Railhead.	a/m
"	11 2/17		Nothing of importance to record. Collected [illegible] Boots + Flapper Pans	a/m
"	12 2/17		Truck of stores arrived at Railhead. collected + distributed to Troops	a/m
"	13 2/17		Refilling 90th Brigade on alternate days at Halloy. Visited Railhead	a/m
"	14 2/17		Visited Amiens on urgent local purchase duties. AA + QMG visited office	a/m
"	15 2/17		DDOS visited office. dump + shops. Truck of stores at Railhead, collected + distributed to Troops	a/m
"	16 2/17		Conference at G office. Truck of stores at Railhead collected + distributed to Troops	a/m

2353 Wt. W2544/1454 700,000 5/15 D. D. & L. A.D.S.S. Forms/C. 2118.

Instructions regarding War Diaries and Intelligence Summaries are contained in F. S. Regs., Part II, and the Staff Manual respectively. Title pages will be prepared in manuscript.

WAR DIARY
or
INTELLIGENCE SUMMARY.
(Erase heading not required.)

2nd Sheet

Army Form C. 2118.

Place	Date	Hour	Summary of Events and Information	Remarks and references to Appendices
BERNEVILLE	17/2/17		Visited Divl School. Truck of 30 Soyers Stoves arrived at Railhead. Visited Doullens for Coal purchase	AMM
"	18/2/17		Order for Lorries to be off the roads enforced until 7am 21st inst.	AMM.
"	19/2/17		Sent unloading party to Railhead, Stores being dumped at a Store near by & will be collected as soon as Motor Transport can remove it. Visited Amiens on urgent Coal purchase	AMM. AMM
"	20/2/17		D.A.Q.M.G. inspected dump & shops.	AMM
"	21/2/17		Train transport collected Ord Stores at Railhead & brought them to the dump, where distributed	AMM
"	22/2/17		Proceeded to Amiens for urgent purchase of Red White Flags	AMM.
"	23/2/17		Impossible to return from Amiens last night owing to state of main roads & dense mist.	AMM
"	24/2/17		Traffic restrictions still being in force, units are unable to draw Ordnance Stores. G.S. Wagons deliver Stores from Railhead	AMM
"	25/2/17		Special Thaw passes obtained for two Brigades of Infantry to draw Ordnance Stores	AMM
"	26/2/17		Thaw restrictions still in force. Dump becoming overloaded with Stores	AMM
"	27/2/17		Obtained Special Pass for four Lorries to proceed to Railhead to collect Stores	AMM
"	28/2/17		Four G. 4.5" Heavy Mortars for W/30 T.M. Bty in formation	AMM

A. M. Mc[illegible] Capt
D.A.D.O.S.
30 Div
28/2/17

2353 Wt. W2544/1454 700,000 5/15 D. D. & L. A.D.S.S. Forms/C 2118

Instructions regarding War Diaries and Intelligence Summaries are contained in F. S. Regs., Part II. and the Staff Manual respectively. Title pages will be prepared in manuscript.

WAR DIARY
or
INTELLIGENCE SUMMARY.

(Erase heading not required.)

Army Form C. 2118.

Vol 17

Place	Date	Hour	Summary of Events and Information	Remarks and references to Appendices
			Confidential War Diary of DADOS 30th Divn From 1st March 1917 To 31st March 1917	

2353 Wt. W2544/1454 700,000 5/15 D. D. & L. A.D.S.S. Forms/C 2118.

Instructions regarding War Diaries and Intelligence Summaries are contained in F. S. Regs., Part II. and the Staff Manual respectively. Title pages will be prepared in manuscript.

WAR DIARY
or
INTELLIGENCE SUMMARY.
(Erase heading not required.)

1st Sheet

Army Form C. 2118.

Place	Date	Hour	Summary of Events and Information	Remarks and references to Appendices
BERNEVILLE	1/3/17		Stores received from Base, collected by Div Train & distributed to units as far as possible	
"	—		in view of Thaw restrictions being still in Force. Visited Amiens for urgent local	
"	—		purchase.	AJM
"	2/3/17		Accompanied DADOS to Laibret to select an Ordnance Dump. Visited Railhead	AJM
"	3/3/17		Moved dump to Railhead to facilitate issues to Troops	AJM
"	4/3/17		A.D.O.S called & visited Shops & dump. Reserves of anti gas appliances to be maintained here	AJM
"	5/3/17		Proceeded to Amiens on Local purchase. Visited dump & Railhead	AJM
"	6/3/17		Visited dump. Stores being issued to Troops normally	AJM
"	7/3/17		DADOS proceeded on leave. 9.45 T. Mortars recently received were without Clinometers, demanding	AJM
"	—		through IV Corps. Sent Chief Clerk to dump.	AJM
"	8/3/17		Visited Amiens & brought stores urgently required for Bombing [illegible]	AJM
"	9/3/17		A.D.O.S visited office & visited dump in afternoon. Issues [illegible] normally	AJM
"	10/3/17		ROO [illegible] wheels at Railhead & [illegible] workshops declined to	
"	—		receive other than serviceable wheels. A.D.O.S taking matter up	AJM
"	11/3/17		Tried without success to proceed to Railhead & dump. Car had to be dug out	
"	—		A.D.O.S visited office.	AJM

2353 Wt. W2544/1454 700,000 5/15 D. D. & L. A.D.S.S. Forms/C. 2118.

Instructions regarding War Diaries and Intelligence Summaries are contained in F. S. Regs., Part II. and the Staff Manual respectively. Title pages will be prepared in manuscript.

WAR DIARY
or
INTELLIGENCE SUMMARY.
(*Erase heading not required.*)

2nd Sheet

Army Form C. 2118.

Place	Date	Hour	Summary of Events and Information	Remarks and references to Appendices
Berneville	12/3/17		Wet weather restrictions again in force. Thaw restrictions enforced again at 9 pm	APM.
"	13/3/17		Sent chief clerk to dump and Railhead. Issues proceeding normally to troops	APM.
"	14/3/17		Visited Railhead & dump. ADOS called in afternoon. Visited D.O.M.	APM
"	15/3/17		Visited dump. Proceeded to Doullens to purchase paint urgently required for grenade boxes	APM
"	16/3/17		G.H.Q. telephoned in response to [illegible] 1/7th Manchester Regt. Visited ADOS, dump & railhead	APM
"	17/3/17		Visited Railhead. Truck in. 18 pdr arrived sent to D.O.M.	APM
"	18/3/17		Two lorries reported under Corps orders to Frevent to collect Tentage & Camp Equipment	APM
"	19/3/17		ADOS visited office. Insisted that DADOS should accompany D.H.Q. on an advance	APM
"	20/3/17		Collected 20 Tarpaulins from Fosseux. Visited dump. Truck cleared. Demanded V.G.	APM
"	21/3/17		Cancelled indent for Vickers gun. ADOS visited dump at Larbret. Visited dump.	APM
"	22/3/17		Detailed lorry to collect salved Ord. Store	APM
"	23/3/17		Truck in at Railhead. Aided Corps Troops to clear their Stores from Railhead	APM
"	24/3/17		Instructed to move to Bretencourt. Visited Railhead & dump.	APM
"	25/3/17		Moved to Bretencourt. Billets re occupied instructed to return to Berneville	APM
"	26/3/17		Moved shops to Bretencourt. Truck in at Railhead. Lorry to workshops, broken down	APM
Bretencourt	27/3/17		Visited Railhead: new unserviceable dump being established quite good	APM

2353 Wt. W2544/1454 700,000 5/15 D. D. & L. A.D.S.S. Forms/C 2118.

Instructions regarding War Diaries and Intelligence Summaries are contained in F. S. Regs., Part II. and the Staff Manual respectively. Title pages will be prepared in manuscript.

WAR DIARY
or
INTELLIGENCE SUMMARY.
(Erase heading not required.)

3 Sheet

Army Form C. 2118.

Place	Date	Hour	Summary of Events and Information	Remarks and references to Appendices
Bretencourt	28/3/17		Cleared truck at Railhead. Visited dump.	APM
"	29/3/17		Visited 'Q'. attended conference at Corps Head Quarters. Visited dump at Laubet	APM
"	30/3/17		attended conference at 'Q' branch. inspected Shops. Found "Special" dump in village	APM
"	31/3/17		Visited dump, railhead + Annexes for local purchase. Refilling units proceeding normally	APM

A P Hewat Captain
D.A.D.O.S.
30th Divn
31/3/17

2353 Wt. W2544/1454 700,000 5/15 D. D. & L. A.D.S.S. Forms/C. 2118.

Instructions regarding War Diaries and Intelligence Summaries are contained in F. S. Regs., Part II. and the Staff Manual respectively. Title pages will be prepared in manuscript.

WAR DIARY
or
INTELLIGENCE SUMMARY.
(Erase heading not required.)

Army Form C. 2118.

Vol 18

Place	Date	Hour	Summary of Events and Information	Remarks and references to Appendices
			Confidential	
			War Diary	
			of	
			D.A.D.O.S.	
			30th Divn.	
			From 1st April 1917 To 30 April 1917	

2353 Wt. W2544/1454 700,000 5/15 D. D. & L. A.D.S.S. Forms/C 2118.

Instructions regarding War Diaries and Intelligence Summaries are contained in F. S. Regs., Part II. and the Staff Manual respectively. Title pages will be prepared in manuscript.

WAR DIARY
or
INTELLIGENCE SUMMARY.
(Erase heading not required.)

1st Sheet

Army Form C. 2118.

Place	Date	Hour	Summary of Events and Information	Remarks and references to Appendices
BRETENCOURT	1/4/17		Wired for 4 Lewis guns for 2nd Yorks. Regt. to replace 1 destroyed by shell fire & 3 captured by the Enemy.	A/M
"	2/4/17		Inspected Divisional Shops. Collected nissen huts & [illegible] for advanced DHQ.	A/M
"	3/4/17		Visited dump & railhead. Refilling of ordnance stores postponed for a day to enable the transport of packsaddlery [illegible] to a forward dump in the village from LARBRET.	A/M
"	4/4/17		Visited dump. 4 Lewis guns arrived for 2nd Yorks. issued them to [illegible] from whom 4 were obtained by Yorks on loan. Anti gas officer visited me. ADOS called	A/M
"	5/4/17		Visited dump & Railhead & proceeded to Amiens for urgent purchase of stores.	A/M
"	6/4/17		Refilled units in the Div. Truck of stores arrived from Base & collected it.	A/M
"	7/4/17		Visited dump. Railhead. Proceeded to Amiens for urgent local purchase	A/M
"	8/4/17		Truck arrived at Railhead. Stores distributed to troops at Refilling point	A/M
"	9/4/17		Visited dump & Railhead. Zero 5 30 am. No instructions recd. that road would be clear	A/M
"	10/4/17		ADOS visited office. detailed 2 Lorries to collect salved stores. 3 Lorries brought from Larbret to stand by in event of DHQ advancing. Visited dump at LARBRET.	A/M
"	11/4/17		Informed by Q that Railhead will change to BOISLEUX-AU-MONT, either tomorrow or next day. Wired for 16 Lewis guns & 1 Vickers to replace casualties.	A/M

2353 Wt. W2544/1454 700,000 5/15 D. D. & L. A.D.S.S. Forms/C. 2118.

Instructions regarding War Diaries and Intelligence Summaries are contained in F. S. Regs., Part II. and the Staff Manual respectively. Title pages will be prepared in manuscript.

WAR DIARY
or
INTELLIGENCE SUMMARY.
(Erase heading not required.)

2nd Sheet

Army Form C. 2118.

Place	Date	Hour	Summary of Events and Information	Remarks and references to Appendices
Bretencourt	12/4/17		Orders to be clear of this village by 4 pm. Impossible. Lent my lorries to DHQ to move	AM
"	13/4/17		Moved to Pommier. Handed over Horseshoes, Buffer Oil & Rifles &c to DADOS 33rd Div	AM.
Pommier	14/4/17		Spoke to ADOS XVIII Corps about Boots shortage & refitting division & if necessary can draw on him for limited quantity of SD & underclothing.	AM.
"	15/4/17		ADOS visited office also Baths & found a large quantity of dirty underclothing left by another division. Having it removed to our Laundry	AM
"	16/4/17		Visited dump with DAQMG & proceeded to Amiens to purchase urgent stores required for refitting Divn. ADOS visited office	AM
"	17/4/17		Visited Railhead & dump at Saulty.	AM
"	18/4/17		Visited Arras to find an office & dump. unsuitable	AM
"	19/4/17		Visited Amiens & brought out flags for Infantry signalling to Artillery	AM
"	20/4/17		Moved to Achicourt. Railhead to Arras. Moved dump to Dainville	AM
Achicourt	21/4/17		ADOS visited dump & office. Visited Salvage dump at Achicourt	AM
"	22/4/17		Established an advance dump at Dainville by Refilling Point	AM
"	23/4/17		Visited Town Major Agny & found Ordnance Stores. advised Salvage.	AM
"	24/4/17		Proceeded to Salvage dump at Neuville Vitasse with Salvage Officer	AM

Instructions regarding War Diaries and Intelligence Summaries are contained in F. S. Regs., Part II. and the Staff Manual respectively. Title pages will be prepared in manuscript.

WAR DIARY
or
INTELLIGENCE SUMMARY.
(Erase heading not required.)

3rd Sheet

Army Form C. 2118.

Place	Date	Hour	Summary of Events and Information	Remarks and references to Appendices
Achicourt	25/4/17		Col Moulton Barrett visited dump at Beaumetz & advanced D.H.Q.	AM
"	26/4/17		Advised by ADOS of relief. Transferred Artillery en bloc to 18th Div	AM
"	27/4/17		Col. Moulton Barrett visited advanced dump at Dainville.	AM
"	28/4/17		Saw Chief Clerk of 18th Div DADOS. pointed out to him Salvage dump locations &c. Preparing to move to ROELLECOURT. Railhead St Pol	AM.
"	29/4/17		Moved to Roellecourt. Shops moving tomorrow.	AM.
Roellecourt	30/4/17		Truck at Railhead. Sent to Beaumetz to clear Blankets	AM.

A.M[illegible] Capt
DADOS
30 Div

30/4/17

2353 Wt. W2544/1454 700,000 5/15 D. D. & L. A.D.S.S. Forms/C. 2118.

Instructions regarding War Diaries and Intelligence Summaries are contained in F. S. Regs., Part II. and the Staff Manual respectively. Title pages will be prepared in manuscript.

WAR DIARY
or
INTELLIGENCE SUMMARY.
(Erase heading not required.)

Army Form C. 2118.

Vol 19

Place	Date	Hour	Summary of Events and Information	Remarks and references to Appendices
			Confidential War Diary of D.A.D.O.S. 30th Divn. From May 1st 917 To May 31st 917.	

2353 Wt. W2544/1454 700,000 5/15 D. D. & L. A.D.S.S. Forms/C 2118.

Instructions regarding War Diaries and Intelligence Summaries are contained in F. S. Regs., Part II. and the Staff Manual respectively. Title pages will be prepared in manuscript.

WAR DIARY
or
~~INTELLIGENCE SUMMARY~~.
(Erase heading not required.)

1st Sheet

Army Form C. 2118.

Place	Date	Hour	Summary of Events and Information	Remarks and references to Appendices
Roellecourt	1/5/17		Truck of stores arrived at Railhead. Carried stores over to 18th Div Dados for 30 Arty	AM
"	2/5/17		Visited 21st Brigade. Stores distributed to troops.	AM
"	3/5/17		Arranged to move to Oeuf - reconsigned trucks to new Railhead	AM
Oeuf	4/5/17		Railhead changed from St Pol to Frevent. Visited 89th Brigade	AM
"	5/5/17		Transferred 30th Artillery from 18th Division & refilling them twice weekly	AM
"	6/5/17		Three trucks of stores arrived at Railhead. Stores distributed to Troops	AM
"	7/5/17		Refilled 89th Brigade. No truck today	AM
"	8/5/17		Refilled 90th Brigade No truck at Railhead.	AM
"	9/5/17		Visited railhead. Two trucks of stores arrived, Stores distributed to Troops	AM
"	10/5/17		Visited Hesdin purchased some stores for issue to the troops.	AM
"	11/5/17		Refilled 89th Brigade. Truck at railhead cleared & stores issued to troops.	AM
"	12/5/17		Visited St Pol. Truck of stores at railhead. Cleared - distributed to Troops.	AM
"	13/5/17		Refilled 90th Brigade. Cleared railhead & issued stores to Troops	AM
"	14/5/17		Visited Willeman & found dump & office. Visited Railhead	AM
"	15/5/17		Moved to Willeman. Two trucks of stores at Railhead cleared to Willeman	AM
Willeman	16/5/17		Refilled 89th Brigade. Visited 21st Bde. H.Qrs	AM
"	17/5/17		Refilled 90th Brigade. Truck of stores at Railhead. Cleared & issued	AM

Army Form C. 2118.

Instructions regarding War Diaries and Intelligence Summaries are contained in F. S. Regs., Part II. and the Staff Manual respectively. Title pages will be prepared in manuscript.

WAR DIARY
or
INTELLIGENCE SUMMARY.
(Erase heading not required.)

2nd Sheet

Place	Date	Hour	Summary of Events and Information	Remarks and references to Appendices
Willeman	18/5/17		Truck of Stores arrived at Railhead. cleared & stores issued to Troops.	AM
"	19/5/17		Refilled 89th Brigade. Truck at Railhead. stores distributed to Troops	AM
"	20/5/17		Refilled 90th Brigade. Reconsigned stores to new area	AM
"	21/5/17		moved to Pernes. Reconsigned two trucks to new Railhead	AM
Pernes	22/5/17		moved to Norrent-Fontes.	AM
Norrent-Fontes	23/5/17		Visited Railhead. RTO cannot reconsign trucks. unloaded & taking by road. Visited DDOS 1st Army at Lillers.	AM
Norrent-Fontes	24/5/17		moved to Steenbecque. Truck of stores at Lillers dumped by RTO.	AM
Steenbecque	25/5/17		D.H.Q. moved to Caestre. Proceeded to R.T.O. Lillers to have truck of stores reconsigned	AM
	26/5/17		Proceeded to Wolau. formed dump. Visited Railhead Wippenhoek	AM
Wolau	27/5/17		Visited DADOS 24th Division & arranged to take over from him.	AM
	28/5/17		Visited ADOS II Corps. 400 Tents sent up from Base unstained.	AM
	29/5/17		arranged move to G.14.b.56. sent up advanced party & delivered stores there.	AM
	30/5/17		Moved to G.14.b.5.4 Sheet 27. Visited Railhead. Visited ADOS 2nd Corps	AM
G.14.b.54	31/5/17		Proceeded to Bailleul & purchased urgent stores: Visited Railhead	AM.

A.M. [illegible] Capt
DADOS 30th Div

2353 Wt. W2544/1454 700,000 5/15 D. D. & L. A.D.S.S./Forms/C. 2118.

Instructions regarding War Diaries and Intelligence Summaries are contained in F. S. Regs., Part II. and the Staff Manual respectively. Title pages will be prepared in manuscript.

WAR DIARY
or
INTELLIGENCE SUMMARY.
(Erase heading not required.)

Army Form C. 2118.

Vol 20

Place	Date	Hour	Summary of Events and Information	Remarks and references to Appendices
			Confidential War Diary of D.A.D.O.S. 50th Div. From 1st June 1917 To 30th June 1917	

2353 Wt. W2544/1454 700,000 5/15 D. D. & L. A.D.S.S. Forms/C. 2118.

Instructions regarding War Diaries and Intelligence Summaries are contained in F. S. Regs., Part II. and the Staff Manual respectively. Title pages will be prepared in manuscript.

WAR DIARY
or
INTELLIGENCE SUMMARY.
(Erase heading not required.)

1st Sheet

Army Form C. 2118.

Place	Date	Hour	Summary of Events and Information	Remarks and references to Appendices
G.14.b.5.4	1/6/17		Truck of Stores received from Base, collected & distributed to Troops.	AM
	2		Visited ADOS and Railhead. proceeded to Bailleul to purchase urgent Stores.	AM
	3		Truck received from Base. Stores distributed to Troops.	AM
	4		Visited 90th Bde at LUMBRES. St OMER Railhead & DDOS L of C North. also Railhead	AM
	5		Sent lorry to XIX Corps to collect 6 Wheels left behind in that area by 89th M.G.C	AM
	6		ADOS called. Truck of stores arrived from Base, cleared & distributed to Tps	AM
	7		Proceeded to Bailleul. Distribution of stores to Troops proceeding normally.	AM
	8		Called on ADOS. Visited Railhead Ordnance Officer at Wippenhoek	AM
	9		Visited Calais Base to talk over Ordnance matters with Base officers.	AM
	10		ADOS called. returned from Calais.	AM
	11		Divl HQrs move from Brandhoek to Reninghelst	AM
	12		Visited Divl H.Qrs. moved from 2nd Army to Fifth Army	AM
	13		moving dump & office to Reninghelst	AM
	14		Tents 120 arrived from Base with cutch. moved stores to Reninghelst	AM
G.30.b.8.10	15		Moved here & opened office at 9 a.m. Railhead moved to G.21.A.6.6.	AM
	16		Visited Railhead. Chief Clerk proceeded on leave.	AM

2353 Wt. W2544/1454 700,000 5/15 D. D. & L. A.D.S.S. Forms/C 2118.

2nd Sheet

Army Form C. 2118.

Instructions regarding War Diaries and Intelligence Summaries are contained in F. S. Regs., Part II. and the Staff Manual respectively. Title pages will be prepared in manuscript.

WAR DIARY
or
INTELLIGENCE SUMMARY.
(Erase heading not required.)

Place	Date	Hour	Summary of Events and Information	Remarks and references to Appendices
G34.c.8.0	17/6/17		Three trucks of stores, including vehicles arrived at Railhead.	AM
	18/6/17		A.D.O.S. moved his office from Steenvoorde to G.16.c.1.7	AM
	19/6/17		Stores arrived from Base & distributed to Troops. ADOS called in morning.	AM
	20/6/17		65 Wheels & 10 Tons General Stores arrived at Railhead. Cleared & issued to Tps	AM
	21/6/17		Truck of stores arrived at Railhead cleared & distributed to Troops.	AM
	22/6/17		Moved 5th RHA ~~FA~~ Bde & 84th RFA Army Bde to XIV C.Tps & 155th RFA Army Bde to XVIII Corps Tps. Truck of General Stores received from Base & issued to Troops.	AM AM
	23/6/17		Two trucks of stores arrived at Railhead, cleared & distributed to Troops	AM
	24/6/17		Visited Railhead & 20th K.L. Regt. Stores being issued to Troops normally.	AM
	25/6/17		Large amount of vehicles being destroyed by shell fire. Service Colour Paint arriving	AM
	26/6/17		Visited Railhead & OO XIV Corps Troops reference outstanding vehicles to 5th RHA Bde	AM
	27/6/17		proceeded to Hazebrouck & purchased few stores urgently required by Troops.	AM
	28/6/17		4 - 9.5 Trench Mortars arriving for this Divn. 2 received at Railhead today	AM
	29/6/17		Two 6" Newton Trench mortars arrived for this Divn. CRA asked for distribution	AM
	30/6/17		Celluloid Sights for Vickers Lewis guns for Anti Aircraft Operations received.	AM

30/6/17. A [illegible] Capt DADOS 30th Divn

2353 Wt. W2544/1454 700,000 5/15 D. D. & L. A.D.S.S. Forms/C. 2118.

Army Form C. 2118.

Instructions regarding War Diaries and Intelligence Summaries are contained in F. S. Regs., Part II. and the Staff Manual respectively. Title pages will be prepared in manuscript.

WAR DIARY
or
INTELLIGENCE SUMMARY.
(Erase heading not required.)

Vol 21

Place	Date	Hour	Summary of Events and Information	Remarks and references to Appendices
			Confidential War Diary ~ of ~ D. A. D. O. S. 30th Divn. From July 1st 1917 To July 31st 1917.	

2353 Wt. W2544/1454 700,000 5/15 D. D. & L. A.D.S.S. Forms/C. 2118.

Instructions regarding War Diaries and Intelligence Summaries are contained in F. S. Regs., Part II. and the Staff Manual respectively. Title pages will be prepared in manuscript.

WAR DIARY
or
INTELLIGENCE SUMMARY.
(Erase heading not required.)

1st Sheet

Army Form C. 2118.

Place	Date	Hour	Summary of Events and Information	Remarks and references to Appendices
G.34.b.8.10 (Reninghelst)	1/7/17		Visited ADOS. 2 Trucks of stores at Railhead.	AJM
	2/7/17		Proceeded to Railhead in the morning. Visited IOM in afternoon.	AJM
	3/7/17		Truck of stores at railhead, cleared & issued to Troops.	AJM
	4/7/17		Visited Hazebrouck & purchased urgent stores. Truck at railhead.	AJM
	5/7/17		Started to move stores to new area. 14 Tons at Railhead to be cleared, cleared.	AJM
	6/7/17		Nothing to report. DAQMG decided that I should not move until tomorrow	AJM
	7/7/17		Moved office to new area, arrived 3pm. No truck at Railhead	AJM
Nordausques	8/7/17		Tried to phone ADOS II Corps to ask whether under II or VIII Corps.	AJM
	9/7/17		Proceeded to St Omer to purchase urgent stores for Troops. No truck in	AJM
	10/7/17		Car at 5 am to take flags to 18th KLRs at Tournehem.	AJM
	11/7/17		ADOS VIII Corps visited office & dump & shops. Found everything satisfactory	AJM
	12/7/17		Truck in at Railhead. Visited St Omer. Sent 2 Lorries to Calais to draw stores.	AJM
	13/7/17		Lorry to Railhead. No truck in. Borrowed store tent & marquee from 11th Div for sports.	AJM
	14/7/17		Lorry to Railhead. Two lorries for leave party. Divisional Sports held in afternoon.	AJM
	15/7/17		DADOS returned from leave. No truck in.	AJM
	16/7/17		Proceeded with Staff Capt "Q" for tour of inspection of Calais Base.	AJM

2353 Wt W2544/1454 700,000 5/15 D. D. & L. A.D.S.S. Forms/C 2118.

Instructions regarding War Diaries and Intelligence Summaries are contained in F. S. Regs., Part II. and the Staff Manual respectively. Title pages will be prepared in manuscript.

WAR DIARY
or
INTELLIGENCE SUMMARY.
(Erase heading not required.)

2nd Sheet.

Army Form C. 2118.

Place	Date	Hour	Summary of Events and Information	Remarks and references to Appendices
Nordasques	17/7		Visited 90th Bde H.Qrs everything satisfactory. Proceeded to Railhead	AJM
	18/7		Proceeded to Calais & obtained all magnetic compasses due to Formation	AJM
Steenvoorde	19/7/16		Two trucks of stores at Railhead, collected distributed to Troops.	AJM
	20/7/16		Visited 16th Manchester Regt. ADOS II Corps & Field Cashier.	AJM
	21/7/16		DADMS inspected Office dump & shops. Visited Hazebrouck in afternoon.	AJM
	22/7/16		Two trucks of stores at Railhead, cleared & distributed to Troops.	AJM
	23/7/16		Proceeded to Reninghelst to inspect [illegible] of 30th Arty attd. to 18th Div.	AJM
	24/7/16		Moved to Reninghelst. & took over dump occupied by 24th Div	AJM
Reninghelst	25/7/16		Proceeded to Hazebrouck to buy Electric Torches required by 21st Bde for special purpose. Attended Conference at ADOS II Corps office.	AJM
	26/7/16		Visited Railhead. Two trucks of stores at Railhead cleared & issued to Troops	AJM
	27/7/16		Visited DDOS Fifth Army & brought back Magnetic Compasses due out	AJM
	28/7/16		DDOS. Fifth Army & Army Salvage officer visited office dump shops & Salvage dump	AJM
	29/7/16		Two trucks at Railhead. cleared & stores distributed to Troops	AJM
	30/7/16		IOM. No 2-16 OMW. called with reference to return of guns to be condemned & replaced, for GOC	AJM
	31/7/16		Visited St. Omer Hazebrouck & Steenvoorde & tried to buy Flat Irons - without success.	AJM

A J M[illegible] Capt
DADOS 30th Div

2353 Wt. W2544/1454 700,000 5/15 D. D. & L. A.D.S.S./Forms/C 2118.

Army Form C. 2118.

Instructions regarding War Diaries and Intelligence Summaries are contained in F. S. Regs., Part II. and the Staff Manual respectively. Title pages will be prepared in manuscript.

WAR DIARY
or
INTELLIGENCE SUMMARY.

(Erase heading not required.)

Vol 22

Place	Date	Hour	Summary of Events and Information	Remarks and references to Appendices
			Confidential	
			War Diary	
			of	
			D.A.D.O.S.	
			30th Div.	
			From August 1st 1917 to 31st August 1917.	

A5834 Wt. W4973/M687 750,000 8/16 D. D. & L. Ltd. Forms/C.2118/13.

Army Form C. 2118.

Instructions regarding War Diaries and Intelligence Summaries are contained in F. S. Regs., Part II. and the Staff Manual respectively. Title pages will be prepared in manuscript.

WAR DIARY
or
INTELLIGENCE SUMMARY.

(Erase heading not required.)

1st Sheet

Place	Date	Hour	Summary of Events and Information	Remarks and references to Appendices
Reninghelst	1 8/17		Visited Railhead. Truck of Stores & G.S. Wagon for this formation, cleared & issued	AMD.
	2 8/17		Visited ADOS 2nd Corps. & I.O.M. Nos 2 & 6.	AMD
	3 8/17		Two trucks of Stores at Railhead. Cleared & distributed to troops	AMD
	4 8/17		Proceeded to Godewaersvelde to find new dump, Office &c	AMD
	5 8/17		Moved to Godewaersvelde - moved from 2nd to 9th Corps in Second Army. Truck at Railhead	AMD
Godewaersvelde	6 8/17		Proceeded to Merris to find new dump, office &c Truck at Railhead	AMD.
	7 8/17		Moved to Merris. Visited ADOS IX Corps with DAQMG	AMD
Merris	8 8/17		A.D.O.S. accompanied by Corps Salvage Offr. visited Office, dump & shops	AMD
	9 8/17		Four trucks of Stores received from Calais. Refitting of Division proceeding	AMD.
	10 8/17		Visited 21st Brigade Headquarters reference to their large refitting indents.	AMD
	11 8/17		Moved to St. Jans Cappel. Visited 21st Bde HQrs reference refitting again.	AMD
St. Jans Cappel	12 8/17		Accompanied by AA&QMG & DAQMG. Visited 89th & 90th Bde HQrs & received refitting indents.	AMD
	13 8/17		ADOS visited Office & dump. Truck of Stores received from Railhead	AMD
	14 8/17		Visited Divl Rest-Camp & inspected a quantity of Ordnance Stores taken over by 98 F. Amb.	AMD
	15 8/17		ADOS visited office. Refitting proceeding rapidly owing to Calais meeting demands quickly	AMD
	16 8/17		Visited Corps H.Q. & Hazebrouck. Visited Baths & Laundry in afternoon	AMD

2353 Wt. W2544/1454 700,000 5/15 D. D. & L. A.D.S.S./Forms/C. 2118.

Instructions regarding War Diaries and Intelligence Summaries are contained in F. S. Regs., Part II. and the Staff Manual respectively. Title pages will be prepared in manuscript.

WAR DIARY
or
INTELLIGENCE SUMMARY.
(Erase heading not required.)

2nd Sheet

Army Form C. 2118.

Place	Date	Hour	Summary of Events and Information	Remarks and references to Appendices
St Jans Cappel	17/8/17		ADOS accompanied by Corps Salvage Officer visited office & discussed method of salvage	APM
	18		Visited Railhead & IOM. 2 Trucks of Stores at Railhead, cleared & distributed.	APM
	19		Visited Dunkerque to try & buy flat irons, only 7 out of 60 available	APM
	20		Visited Dranoutre where we take over from 4th Australian Division	APM
	21		Proceeded to Railhead, visited DOM. Truck of stores at Railhead	APM
	22		ADOS called & inspected dump & Shoemakers Shop.	APM
	23		Moved to Dranoutre, completed transference of Stores from St Jans Cappel	APM
Dranoutre	24		18 Tons of Stores at Railhead, cleared by midday, & distributed as far as possible to Corps	APM
	25		18pdr Carriage & Cart Water Tank at Railhead for Artillery, units asked to collect —	APM
	26		Nothing to report. DADMS visited office & dump.	APM
	27		Nine tons General Stores at Railhead, cleared & distributed to troops.	APM
	28		DADOS 4th Australian Div called regarding transfer of their Artillery to this formation	APM
	29		Store tent blown down & torn to shreds as result of a gale. 2 Vehicles at Railhead	APM
	30		13 Tons of General Stores at Railhead, cleared & issued to units	APM
	31		Orders for camouflage material for tents in the area, wired base for requirements	APM

A.P. Murmel Capt
DADOS 30th Div

2353 Wt. W2544/1454 700,000 5/15 D. D. & L. A.D.S.S. Forms/C. 2118.

Instructions regarding War Diaries and Intelligence Summaries are contained in F. S. Regs., Part II. and the Staff Manual respectively. Title pages will be prepared in manuscript.

WAR DIARY
or
INTELLIGENCE SUMMARY.
(Erase heading not required.)

Army Form C. 2118.

Vol 23

Place	Date	Hour	Summary of Events and Information	Remarks and references to Appendices
			Confidential War Diary of D.A.D.O.S. 30th Divn From 1st Septr 1917 To 30th Septr 1917	

A5834 Wt. W4973/M687 750,000 8/16 D. D. & L. Ltd. Forms/C.2118/13.

Instructions regarding War Diaries and Intelligence Summaries are contained in F. S. Regs., Part II. and the Staff Manual respectively. Title pages will be prepared in manuscript.

WAR DIARY
or
INTELLIGENCE SUMMARY.
(Erase heading not required.)

1st Sheet.

Army Form C. 2118.

Place	Date	Hour	Summary of Events and Information	Remarks and references to Appendices
Dranoutre	1/9/17		Sent lorry to Calais to collect 3 cwt of Cutch urgently required in the area	[illegible]
	2/9/17		Eight tons of Stores at Railhead, cleared & distributed. Lorry returned from Calais	[illegible]
	3/9/17		Truck with 40 Bicycles at Railhead, replacing horses.	[illegible]
	4/9/17		Visited Railhead, complaints of unserviceable clothing being returned in Sandbags.	[illegible]
	5/9/17		Visited 21st Brigade Headquarters. DAQMG visited dump & shops	[illegible]
	6/9/17		Visited 10M and Railhead. Trucks unloaded & cleared normally	[illegible]
	7/9/17		Conference at office of ADOS. Visited laundry in afternoon	[illegible]
	8/9/17		Visited Railhead; arranged for use of Disinfector for S.D. Clothing, [illegible]	[illegible]
	9/9/17		No truck in today. Visited Salvage dump in company with Salvage officer [illegible]	[illegible]
	10/9/17		Visited ADOS. Visited 89th Brigade Head Qrs. demand [illegible] for 2nd Bedfords	[illegible]
	11/9/17		proceeded to 97th Field Ambulance & Supply Column	[illegible]
	12/9/17		Proceeded to Railhead. wired for 14000 Blankets [illegible] of 1 per man	[illegible]
	13/9/17		No truck at Railhead today. AA & QMG visited dump	[illegible]
	14/9/17		ADOS called. Truck of stores & amm[n] wagon at Railhead	[illegible]
	15/9/17		Two trucks of stores at Railhead. Blankets [illegible] & [illegible] issued.	[illegible]
	16/9/17		DDOS 2nd Army inspected dump office shops & mens kitchen. all satisfactory	[illegible]

2353 Wt. W2544/1454 700,000 5/15 D. D. & L. A.D.S.S. Forms/C. 2118.

Instructions regarding War Diaries and Intelligence Summaries are contained in F. S. Regs., Part II. and the Staff Manual respectively. Title pages will be prepared in manuscript.

WAR DIARY
or
INTELLIGENCE SUMMARY.
(*Erase heading not required.*)

2nd Sheet

Army Form C. 2118.

Place	Date	Hour	Summary of Events and Information	Remarks and references to Appendices
Dranoutre	17/9/17		No truck at Railhead today. Visited I.O.M. and 201 Field Co. RE.	G.M.
	18		A.D.O.S called & inspected dump & shops.	G.M.
	19		New system of Ordnance Train not a success. [i.e. Armourers shop	G.M.
	20		Railhead changed to BRULOOZE. Not sufficient M. guns being received for overhaul ^	G.M.
	21		Wired to Corps complaining of the new Ordnance train as wholly unsatisfactory.	G.M.
	22		Moved into VIII Corps from IX Corps. Visited Railhead.	G.M.
	23		Sent letter to Arty. H.Qrs complaining of unsatisfactory return of S.D. Clothing from Arty. units	G.M.
	24		Received copy of letter sent out by C.R.A. reference return of S.D. Clothing	G.M.
	25		Nothing to report. Conference of Staff Captains, Q.M.'s & Q.M.S.'s at Div. H.Qrs	G.M.
	26		Two trucks received at Railhead. Railhead changed from Brulooze to Hagedoorn	G.M.
	27		Proceeded to 21st Bde H.Qrs together with Div. Salvage Officer	G.M.
	28		Visited Second Army Sniping School. 49th Artillery transferred to V Corps.	G.M.
	29		Visited Ouderdom & Hagedoorn Railheads. No truck from Base.	G.M.
	30		Corps Salvage Officer called on me with reference to disposal of stores likely to meet outstanding indents of this formation.	G.M.

G.M. [signature] Capt
DADOS
30th Div
30/9/17.

2353 Wt. W2544/1454 700,000 5/15 D. D. & L. A.D.S.S. Forms/C. 2118.

Instructions regarding War Diaries and Intelligence Summaries are contained in F. S. Regs., Part II. and the Staff Manual respectively. Title pages will be prepared in manuscript.

WAR DIARY
or
INTELLIGENCE SUMMARY.

(Erase heading not required.)

Army Form C. 2118.

Vol 24

Place	Date	Hour	Summary of Events and Information	Remarks and references to Appendices
			Confidential War Diary of DADOS 30th Divn From 1st October 1917 To 31st October 1917.	

2353 Wt. W2544/1454 700,000 5/15 D. D. & L. A.D.S.S. Forms/C. 2118.

Army Form C. 2118.

WAR DIARY
or
INTELLIGENCE SUMMARY.
(*Erase heading not required.*)

1st Sheet

Instructions regarding War Diaries and Intelligence Summaries are contained in F. S. Regs., Part II. and the Staff Manual respectively. Title pages will be prepared in manuscript.

Place	Date	Hour	Summary of Events and Information	Remarks and references to Appendices
Dranoutre	1/10/17		Visited 89th Bde H.Q. and 97th Field Ambulance	AM
	2/10/17		Staff Captain 21st Bde visited me, Everything satisfactory with units in his Brigade.	AM
	3/10/17		Report from 18th KLR. that Blankets recently issued, were issued in verminous condition found [to be unfounded, the lice being apparently caught in the trenches]	AM
	4/10/17		F. S. Boots arrived from Base	AM
	5/10/17		Body Bands, Waistcoats Cardigan, Cap Comforters. Worsted Gloves & Woollen Vests received from Base	AM
	6/10/17		Sent supplementary indent for Winter clothing to Base (in accordance with Winter Scale	AM
	7/10/17		Demanded Tools & repairing outfit for repairs to Gum Boots. Five trucks from Base.	AM
	8/10/17		Visited Railhead at Haagedoorne demanded 50 Soyers Stoves from Base	AM
	9/10/17		Demanded 400 Braziers from Base. Visited 20th Kings L Regt. No truck from Base	AM
	10/10/17		Visited 90th Bde H.Q. 21st Bde coming out of line apply for Armourers for overhaul work.	AM
	11/10/17		Two trucks of stores from Base.	AM
	12/10/17		Visited railhead & Bailleul for local purchase	AM
	13/10/17		Asked A.D.O.S. when Horse Rugs were likely to be approved for issue. Horse clipping starts [15th Oct]	AM
	14/10/17		Loaned 160 Horse Rugs to 33rd Division as their horse clipping is in progress.	AM
	15/10/17		A.D.O.S. visited office dump Shops also 'Q' branch.	AM
	16/10/17		No truck today. Loaned further 100 Horse Rugs to 33rd Div. This Div clipping [not yet commencing]	AM

2353 Wt. W2544/1454 700,000 5/15 D. D. & L. A.D.S.S. Forms/C 2118.

Instructions regarding War Diaries and Intelligence Summaries are contained in F. S. Regs., Part II. and the Staff Manual respectively. Title pages will be prepared in manuscript.

WAR DIARY
or
INTELLIGENCE SUMMARY.
(Erase heading not required.)

2nd Sheet

Army Form C. 2118.

Place	Date	Hour	Summary of Events and Information	Remarks and references to Appendices
Dramontré	17/10/17		Indented for 400 Braziers in accordance with GRO 2705 d/ 10th Oct.	[illegible]
	18/10/17		D.A.Q.M.G. visited dump & office.	[illegible]
	19/10/17		Indented for Leather Jerkins for Infantry. No truck in today	[illegible]
	20/10/17		Two trucks from Base. Cleared & stores distributed to troops	[illegible]
	21/10/17		Visited Amiens for urgent purchase of materials for Trench Feet.	[illegible]
	22/10/17		Proceeded to Railhead. Nothing of importance to report.	[illegible]
	23/10/17		2nd Blanket per man arrived from Base. 400 Braziers also received	[illegible]
	24/10/17		Horse Rugs arrived from Base.	[illegible]
	25/10/17		Two trucks General stores arrived from Base. No Vouchers or Waybills. [illegible]	[illegible]
	26/10/17		Refitted [illegible] units in forward area. Visit from A DOS. All satisfactory	[illegible]
	27/10/17		Lorry sent to Calais for Paillasses. Nothing else of importance to report	[illegible]
	28/10/17		Truck of stores from Base. Cleared and distributed.	[illegible]
	29/10/17		Truck from Base General stores. [illegible]	[illegible]
	30/10/17		3 trucks [illegible] at Railhead. Cleared [illegible]	[illegible]
	31/10/17		Refitted [illegible]	[illegible]

[illegible] Capt
DADOS
30th Div

2353 Wt. W2544/1454 700,000 5/15 D. D. & L. A.D.S.S./Forms/C. 2118.

Army Form C. 2118.

Instructions regarding War Diaries and Intelligence Summaries are contained in F. S. Regs., Part II. and the Staff Manual respectively. Title pages will be prepared in manuscript.

WAR DIARY
or
INTELLIGENCE SUMMARY.
(Erase heading not required.)

Vol 25

Place	Date	Hour	Summary of Events and Information	Remarks and references to Appendices
			— Confidential —	
			War Diary	
			of	
			D.A.D.O.S.	
			30th Divn	
			From 1st Novr 1917 to 30th Novr 1917.	

2353 Wt. W2544/1454 700,000 5/15 D. D. & L. A.D.S.S. Forms/C 2118.

Instructions regarding War Diaries and Intelligence Summaries are contained in F. S. Regs., Part II. and the Staff Manual respectively. Title pages will be prepared in manuscript.

WAR DIARY
or
INTELLIGENCE SUMMARY.

(Erase heading not required.)

1st Sheet

Army Form C. 2118.

Place	Date	Hour	Summary of Events and Information	Remarks and references to Appendices
Dranoutre	1 NOV 17		9 Trucks of tent bottoms at Railhead. 1 truck of F.S. Boots. cleared & issued	[illegible]
"	2/11/17		8 tons General Stores cleared from Railhead & issued to troops	[illegible]
"	3/11/17		5 Trucks at Railhead. tent bottoms, Special Winter Tins, Undercoats fur, Cases Paillasse & Washing Tubs	[illegible]
"	4/11/17		2 Trucks of general stores cleared from Railhead & issued to Troops	[illegible]
"	5/11/17		1 Truck of Horse Rugs + 1 of tent bottoms. visited Railhead thence to Bailleul to purchase stores	[illegible]
"	6/11/17		1 Truck of General Stores & one vehicle cleared from Railhead & issued.	[illegible]
"	7/11/17		Nothing special to report. everything normal. Sent lorry to Corps Tps for stores for attd. units	[illegible]
"	8/11/17		1 Truck of general stores & one gun for 104 AFA Bde at Railhead. cleared & issued	[illegible]
"	9/11/17		2 Trucks of general stores & clothing cleared from Railhead & issued to troops	[illegible]
"	10/11/17		2 Vehicles at Railhead. Units wired to collect. Lt Edwards arrived from Boulogne	[illegible]
"	11/11/17		Visited Steenvoorde & looked for dump & shops. unsuccessful.	[illegible]
"	12/11/17		Again visited Steenvoorde & found accomodation which is bad.	[illegible]
"	13/11/17		Visited Salvage Dump & explained method of Salvage to Lieut Edwards.	[illegible]
"	14/11/17		Visited Railhead & new area with Lieut Edwards.	[illegible]
"	15/11/17		Visited 89th Bde. H.Qs & 20th Kings. DAQMG. visited dump.	[illegible]
"	16/11/17		Three trucks of stores arrived at Railhead. cleared & distributed to Troops	[illegible]

2353 Wt. W2544/1454 700,000 5/15 D. D. & L. A.D.S.S. Forms/C. 2118.

Army Form C. 2118.

Instructions regarding War Diaries and Intelligence Summaries are contained in F. S. Regs., Part II. and the Staff Manual respectively. Title pages will be prepared in manuscript.

WAR DIARY
or
INTELLIGENCE SUMMARY.

(Erase heading not required.)

Place	Date	Hour	Summary of Events and Information	Remarks and references to Appendices
Steenvoorde	17/4/17		Moved from Dranoutre. One truck of stores at new Railhead Wippenhoek.	AM
	18		visited Railhead & I.O.M. no truck today. DADMS & AA & QMG visited dump	AM
	19		Two trucks of stores received from Base. Cleared & distributed	AM
	20		Lieut Edwards returned to Boulogne. no truck at Railhead today	AM
	21		proceeded to Calais to arrange visit of GOC 89th Bde	AM
	22		Accompanied G.O.C. 89th Bde to Calais. DADOS 39th Div came to see store &	AM
	23		went to Dranoutre to see 39th Div Ordce dump & shops. taking over 27th inst	AM
	24		nothing to report everything proceeding normally.	AM
	25		Two trucks of stores at Railhead. cleared & distributed to troops.	AM
	26		transferred stores & shops from Dranoutre to Westoutre.	AM
Westoutre	27		moved to Westoutre into IX Corps. new Railhead at Dickebusch	AM
	28		proceeded to Railhead. Truck of stores at Railhead cleared & issued	AM
	29		One truck & 1 limbered wagon at Railhead, cleared & collected.	AM
	30		Lorried out stores to Gunners & Field Coys in the line.	AM.

A.M. Mummel [?]
Capt
DADOS 30th Div

2353 Wt. W2534/1454 700,000 5/15 D. D. & L. A.D.S.S. Forms/C 2118.

Instructions regarding War Diaries and Intelligence Summaries are contained in F. S. Regs., Part II. and the Staff Manual respectively. Title pages will be prepared in manuscript.

WAR DIARY
or
INTELLIGENCE SUMMARY.
(Erase heading not required.)

Army Form C. 2118.

Vol 26

Place	Date	Hour	Summary of Events and Information	Remarks and references to Appendices
			— Confidential —	
			War Diary	
			of	
			D.A.D.O.S. 30th Div	
			from 1/12/17 to 31/12/17.	

2353 Wt. W2544/1454 700,000 5/15 D. D. & L. A.D.S.S. Forms/C. 2118.

Instructions regarding War Diaries and Intelligence Summaries are contained in F. S. Regs., Part II. and the Staff Manual respectively. Title pages will be prepared in manuscript.

WAR DIARY
or
INTELLIGENCE SUMMARY.
(Erase heading not required.)

Army Form C. 2118.

1st Sheet

Place	Date	Hour	Summary of Events and Information	Remarks and references to Appendices
Westoutre	1/12/17		Visited ADOS at IX Corps H.Qrs. visited 89th Bde HQrs in the afternoon.	AM
"	2/12/17		German Minenwerfer claimed by 89th Bde handed into dump.	AM
"	3/12/17		Visited Amiens to purchase necessary ingredients for making Trench Foot Powder	AM
"	4/12/17		Returned from Amiens. Supervised packing of Unserviceable Clothing & Stores.	AM
"	5/12/17		Demanded Vickers gun for 89th Machine Gun Company. Visited 96 Field Ambce	AM
"	6/12/17		A.D.O.S. IX Corps visited dump, office, shops, [illegible] afterwards Q branch	AM
"	7/12/17		D/148 demanded 4.5 Howitzer. Visited 90th Bde Mach. Gun. Coy	AM
"	8/12/17		Demanded Lewis gun for 2nd Wiltshire Regiment to replace one damaged by shell	AM
"	9/12/17		Visited Railhead. Visited Divl. Mach. Gun Officer in afternoon.	AM
"	10/12/17		Ten thousand Paillasses received from Base. Visited 21st Bde H.Qrs	AM
"	11/12/17		89th Bde submit their claim for minenwerfer handed in on 2nd inst.	AM
"	12/12/17		Visited 2 Section DAC & Nos 2 & 4 Coys 30 Div Train. Valued Chaffcutters.	AM.
"	13/12/17		Visited B/148 Bde RFA & valued chaffcutter. Truck of stores at Railhead	AM
"	14/12/17		Two trucks of stores at Railhead Cleared & distributed to troops.	AM
"	15/12/17		Visited Railhead. nothing to report. Demanded 3 Lewis guns for 21 MGC.	AM
"	16/12/17		Visited Mob. Veterinary Section & 89th Bde H.qrs. Demanded Lewis gun for 18th [illegible]	AM

Instructions regarding War Diaries and Intelligence Summaries are contained in F. S. Regs., Part II. and the Staff Manual respectively. Title pages will be prepared in manuscript.

WAR DIARY
or
INTELLIGENCE SUMMARY.
(Erase heading not required.)

2nd Sheet

Army Form C. 2118.

Place	Date	Hour	Summary of Events and Information	Remarks and references to Appendices
WESTOUTRE	17 12/17		Demanded 9 Lewis Guns for 18th MCW. to replace others lost to the enemy	AM
"	18 12/17		A.D.O.S. visited office dump & shops. accompanied him to Q office.	AM
"	19 12/17		Received 300 Suits of S.D. Clothing authorized under Q.M.G. 4/12 (Q.A.3) of 9.2.17	AM
"	20 12/17		Fourth Army took over from Second Army from this date	AM
"	21 12/17		Visited by American General & his staff. Explained Ordnance Services with a Division	AM
"	22 12/17		Tables & Forms urgently demanded by units in huts.	AM
"	23 12/17		C.I.O.M. Fourth Army visited Armourers Shop & see Vickers Gun Bolts.	AM
"	24 12/17		Wired for 180 suits of White drill for raiding purposes. urgently required on account of Snow	AM
"	25 12/17		Explained Ordnance Services with a Division to two Q (Officers) Course.	AM
"	26 12/17		ADOS IX Corps visited office & stores.	AM
"	27 12/17		Two trucks of stores at Railhead, cleared & distributed to troops	AM
"	28 12/17		Nothing to report. everything normally going on	AM
"	29 12/17		Forms & Tables received from Base. Distributed to Area Commandants.	AM
"	30 12/17		Proceeded to Calais to shew over Salvage dump & workshops to 60 officers & 49 O.R. of this Div.	AM
"	31 12/17		Returned from Calais. G.O.C. visited Office.	AM

[illegible] Capt
DADOS 30th Div.

2353 Wt W2534/1454 700,000 5/15 D. D. & L. A.D.S.S. Forms/C. 2118.

Instructions regarding War Diaries and Intelligence Summaries are contained in F. S. Regs., Part II. and the Staff Manual respectively. Title pages will be prepared in manuscript.

WAR DIARY
or
INTELLIGENCE SUMMARY.
(Erase heading not required.)

Army Form C. 2118.

Vol 27

Place	Date	Hour	Summary of Events and Information	Remarks and references to Appendices
			Confidential	
			War Diary	
			of	
			D.A.D.O.S. 30th Division	
			From January 1st 1918 – To January 31st 1918	

2353 Wt. W2544/1454 700,000 5/15 D. D. & L. A.D.S.S./Forms/C. 2118.

Instructions regarding War Diaries and Intelligence Summaries are contained in F. S. Regs., Part II. and the Staff Manual respectively. Title pages will be prepared in manuscript.

WAR DIARY
or
INTELLIGENCE SUMMARY.
(*Erase heading not required.*)

1st Sheet.

Army Form C. 2118.

Place	Date Jany 1918	Hour	Summary of Events and Information	Remarks and references to Appendices
Westoutre	1		A.D.O.S IX Corps called at office and inspected dump & shops	AM
	2		D.A.D.O.S. 20th Div^n visited me in connection with taking over from this Division	AM
	3		Attended conference at IX Corps H.Q^s reference Artillery "cycle" of handing over	AM
	4		Visited 20th Div^n area & D.A.D.O.S at Blaringhem & arranged handing over stores re	AM
	5		Indented for 8. 18pdrs for arty deficient in taking over 4th Australian Div guns	AM
	6		Moved to Blaringhem en route for Corbie. (5th Army area) detrained at Longeau	AM
Blaringhem	7		Visited Ebblinghem Railhead & arranged for trucks to send stores to VILLERS BRETONNEUX	AM
	8		made all arrangements for prospective move tomorrow	AM.
	9		moved to Corbie - proceeded by train. sent personnel by lorries	AM
Corbie	10		arrived at Corbie. Truck of Horseshoes, oil & grease at Railhead. Cleared it.	AM.
	11		Two trucks containing accumulated stores despatched from Ebblinghem arrived. cleared.	AM.
	12		went to Roye with D.A.A.G. & visited R.A. H.Q. reference query whether B.M.s required for 8 guns	AM.
	13		visited the 3 Infantry Brigade H.Q^s. A.D.O.S. XVIII Corps visited office	AM
Nesle	14		moved to NESLE by rail. Lorries & personnel by road.	AM
	15		Thaw restrictions came into force.	AM
	16		Visited 90th B^de H.Q^s & M. Gun. Coy. Everything satisfactory	AM
	17		Visited Amiens to purchase Blowlamps. obtained 10 with considerable difficulty	AM
	18		wire received sanctioning issue of 8. 18pdr guns from No 3 Army Gun Park	AM
	19		Div^l H.Q^s moved to Ercheu owing to Thaw restrictions I cannot move until tomorrow	AM.
Ercheu	20		moved to Ercheu. cleared part of dump at Nesle	AM
	21		Thaw restrictions removed. cleared remainder of dump at Nesle	AM
	22		Visited Div^l Supply Column. received books & indents of Div^l Troops & artillery	AM
	23		G.O.C. R.A. visited office to enquire of position regarding indents of artillery	AM.
	24		8. 18 pdrs advised as despatched by 3 Ord Gun Park to Nesle	AM

8353 Wt. W2544/1454 700,000 5/15 D. D. & L. A.D.S.S./Forms/C. 2118.

Army Form C. 2118.

Instructions regarding War Diaries and Intelligence Summaries are contained in F. S. Regs., Part II. and the Staff Manual respectively. Title pages will be prepared in manuscript.

WAR DIARY
or
INTELLIGENCE SUMMARY.
(Erase heading not required.)

2nd Sheet.

Place	Date	Hour	Summary of Events and Information	Remarks and references to Appendices
	Jan. 1918			
Erchen	25		8. 18 pdrs at Nesle Railhead. Advised Arty for immediate removal of them	AMO.
	26		Sent part of Stores to new area. made arrangements to collect trench stores from O.O. III Corps Troops at Flavy le Martel - which will have to be delivered to Bde H.Qrs at night.	AMO.
	27		Sent remainder of Stores with Exception of Office to ~~CHAUNY~~ OGNES. now in III Corps	AMO.
	28		Moved to CHAUNY with Divl H.Qrs	
CHAUNY	29		visited dump at Ognes. Lorried out Hotfood Containers to Bdes. H.Qrs	AMO.
	30		5 Trucks of Trench Stores at O.O. III Corps Tps. visited dump at Ognes.	AMO.
	31		Moved to Ognes owing to Enemy bombing of Chauny.	AMO.

[signature] Capt
D.A.D.O.S.
30th Divn
31/1/1918.

2353 Wt. W2544/1454 700,000 5/15 D. D. & L. A.D.S.S./Forms/C. 2118.

Instructions regarding War Diaries and Intelligence Summaries are contained in F. S. Regs., Part II. and the Staff Manual respectively. Title pages will be prepared in manuscript.

WAR DIARY
or
~~INTELLIGENCE~~ SUMMARY.
(Erase heading not required.)

1st Sheet.

Army Form C. 2118.

DADOS 30 D

Vol 28

Place	Date	Hour	Summary of Events and Information	Remarks and references to Appendices
Ognes	1 2/18		Refilled Artillery Field Companies + Pioneers. 2 Trucks at Railhead	AM
	2 2/18		visited 21st Bde H.Qrs reference disbanding of 19th Manch. Regiment	AM
	3 2/18		visited 89th Bde H.Qrs reference disbanding of 20th K. L'pool regiment	AM
	4 2/18		visited 90th Bde H.Qrs reference disbanding of 18th Manch. Regiment	AM
	5 2/18		visited Artillery H.Qrs at Offoy visited 96th Field Ambulance	AM
	6 2/18		Receiving stores of disbanded Battalions excepting 16th Manch Regt who are in the line	AM
	7 2/18		Visited Railhead, Pioneer Battn + 200th Field Coy.	AM
	8 2/18		proceeded to new area to take over same dump + office as before.	AM
Erchen	9 2/18		moved to Erchen in XVIII Corps. Nothing to report otherwise.	AM
	10 2/18		A.D.O.S. visited office + stores. accompanied him to 'Q' reference supply of Shrinkage	AM
	11 2/18		Staff Capt 89th Bde visited me reference stores for Brigade School of Instruction	AM
	12 2/18		Proceeded to HAM + visited ADOS XVIII Corps. visited Railhead returning.	AM
	13 2/18		Refilled Field Companies + Pioneers. Visited Divl Supply Column.	AM
	14 2/18		A.A.+QMG + DAQMG visited dumps. visited 89th Bde HQrs in afternoon.	AM
	15 2/18		Collected Tents from Fifth Army Troops No1. for Battn doing road work at CHAULNES	AM
	16 2/18		Sent by rail 9 Rifles with Telescopic Sights to Sniping School from disbanded Battalions	AM
	17 2/18		Collected 600 sets of underclothing + delivered to the 11th 8th Lancs at DURY	AM
	18 2/18		Sent to O.O. XVIII Corps Troops + drew 20 Tents for 18th Manchester Regt at CHAULNES	AM
	19 2/18		Assistant Inspector of Armourers visited Divisional Armourers Shop	AM
	20 2/18		Warned that Thaw precautions will probably be enforced at 6 pm tomorrow	AM
	21 2/18		Thaw precautions adopted. arranged to dump older stores at Railhead + leave a lorry there	AM

2353 Wt. W2544/1454 700,000 5/15 D. D. & L. A.D.S.S./Forms/C. 2118.

Army Form C. 2118.

Instructions regarding War Diaries and Intelligence Summaries are contained in F. S. Regs., Part II, and the Staff Manual respectively. Title pages will be prepared in manuscript.

WAR DIARY

or

~~INTELLIGENCE~~ SUMMARY.

(*Erase heading not required.*)

2nd Sheet.

Place	Date	Hour	Summary of Events and Information	Remarks and references to Appendices
Erchen	22/2/18		Instructions to move to HAM. cancelled owing to thaw restrictions	APD.
	23/2/18		Moved to HAM. excepting for Stores which owing to thaw restrictions are left behind	APD.
HAM	24/2/18		Truck at Railhead. Stores placed on dump ~~????~~ near Railhead.	LB
	25/2/18		Visited new area to inspect dumps preparatory to moving	LB
DURY	26/2/18		Moved to DURY. Thaw restrictions removed.	LB
	27/2/18		Moved stores from dump at Railhead to new dumps.	LB
	28/2/18		Truck at Railhead cleared and stores distributed.	LB

L. E. Fullerton [?] Lieut. for Captain
D.A.D.O.S.
"30th Div"

1/2/18

2353 Wt. W2544/1454 700,000 5/15 D. D. & L. A.D.S.S./Forms/C. 2118.

Instructions regarding War Diaries and Intelligence Summaries are contained in F. S. Regs., Part II. and the Staff Manual respectively. Title pages will be prepared in manuscript.

WAR DIARY
or
INTELLIGENCE SUMMARY.
(Erase heading not required.)

Vol 29

Army Form C. 2118.

Place	Date	Hour	Summary of Events and Information	Remarks and references to Appendices
			Confidential War Diary of D.A.D.O.S. 30th Div. from 1 – 3. 18 to 31. 3. 18.	

2353 Wt. W2544/1454 700,000 5/15 D. D. & L. A.D.S.S./Forms/C. 2118.

Army Form C. 2118.

Instructions regarding War Diaries and Intelligence Summaries are contained in F. S. Regs., Part II. and the Staff Manual respectively. Title pages will be prepared in manuscript.

WAR DIARY
or
INTELLIGENCE SUMMARY.
(Erase heading not required.)

1st Sheet

Place	Date	Hour	Summary of Events and Information	Remarks and references to Appendices
DURY.	1.3.18		ADOS visited new dump Inspected Shops. Everything in order	
	2.		Truck at Railhead Horseshoes. Distributed to Units.	
	3.		Visited Italian Labour Company. Inspected Camp and estimated their urgent requirements	
	4		Railhead changes to Villers St Christophe. Arranged to still send [illegible] stores to HAM	
	5		Also attended Economy lecture given Major – AOD at HAM.	
	6.		Two trucks at Railhead. Cleared and stores distributed	
	7		Truck General stores and truck area stores, forms tables etc. Both cleared. Area stores delivered	
	8		Truck Vehicles at Railhead. Units wired to clear.	
			[illegible] from Railhead. Visit [illegible] Italian Camp.	
	10		Truck containing general stores and area stores. Latter delivered to Area Commdts	
	11		Nothing to report	
	12		No truck in. Visited 21st Bde. Found everything in order. Visited Italian Camp.	
	13.		DDOS Fifth Army and ADOS XVIII Corps visited dump. Everything satisfactory.	
	14		Truck at Railhead cleared and distributed	
	15		ADR [illegible] dump. Brought 300 2" T.M. Fuses for modification in Armourers Shop	
	16		300 Fuses completed. C.R.E. to draw.	
	17		600 [illegible] 200 sets underclothing drawn from Corps to Baths for use in gas cases	
	18		All [illegible] [illegible] Divl Shop from Bdes and [illegible]. Truck cleared from Railhead.	
	19		Obtained and delivered 600 suits Service D. clothing to Divl Baths.	
	20		Truck cleared from Railhead. Obtained [illegible] Baths	

2353 Wt. W2544/1454 700,000 5/15 D. D. & L. A.D.S.S./Forms/C. 2118.

Instructions regarding War Diaries and Intelligence Summaries are contained in F. S. Regs., Part II. and the Staff Manual respectively. Title pages will be prepared in manuscript.

WAR DIARY
or
INTELLIGENCE SUMMARY.
(Erase heading not required.)

2nd Sheet.

Army Form C. 2118.

Place	Date	Hour	Summary of Events and Information	Remarks and references to Appendices
DURY	21.		[illegible]	
	22.		[illegible] Remainder destroyed.	
	23.		[illegible] Returned to Base.	
	24.		[illegible]	
	25.		[illegible]	
	26.		[illegible] wagons [illegible] not available. Remained loaded.	
	26.		[illegible]	
	27.		[illegible]	
	28.		[illegible]	
	29.		[illegible]	
	29.		[illegible]	
	30.		[illegible]	
	31.		[illegible]	

[illegible] Major.

2353 Wt. W2544/1454 700,000 5/15 D. D. & L. A.D.S.S./Forms/C. 2118.

Army Form C. 2118.

Instructions regarding War Diaries and Intelligence Summaries are contained in F. S. Regs., Part II. and the Staff Manual respectively. Title pages will be prepared in manuscript.

WAR DIARY
or
INTELLIGENCE SUMMARY.

(Erase heading not required.)

Vol 30

Place	Date	Hour	Summary of Events and Information	Remarks and references to Appendices
			Confidential War Diary 2 D.A.D.O.S. 30th Div from 1 - 4 - 18 to 30 - 4 - 18.	

2353 Wt. W2544/1454 700,000 5/15 D. D. & L. A.D.S.S./Forms/C. 2118.

Instructions regarding War Diaries and Intelligence Summaries are contained in F. S. Regs., Part II. and the Staff Manual respectively. Title pages will be prepared in manuscript.

WAR DIARY
or
INTELLIGENCE SUMMARY.
(Erase heading not required.)

1st Sheet

Army Form C. 2118.

Place	Date	Hour	Summary of Events and Information	Remarks and references to Appendices
St Valery S/S	1/4/18		Moved in from Saleux. DDOS L of C visited office	AJO
	2/4/18		Lt Col Exham from GHQ visited HQrs to know state of Ordnance with Divn	AJO
	3/4/18		demanded 144 Lewis guns & 44 Vickers to refit Divn	AJO
Proven	4/4/18		Moved to Proven. Change of Base from Havre to Calais	AJO
	5/4/18		cancelled indents on 5th Army Gun Park & resubmitted on 2nd Army G.P.	AJO
	6/4/18		Received 20 Lewis guns & 12 Vickers from II Corps on account of indent	AJO
	7/4/18		Received remainder of guns. Visited A.D.O.S. II Corps H.Q.	AJO
	8/4/18		Moved to Elverdinghe. Railhead Ordnance Officer called on me	AJO
Elverdinghe	9/4/18		Visited 89th Bde H.Qrs with A.A.&Q.M.G. & investigated mach. gun position	AJO
	10/4/18		Visited 90th Bde H.Qrs reference their demands for machine guns	AJO
	11/4/18		ADOS visited dump. Visited 21st Bde reference machine guns.	AJO
	12/4/18		Stopped issues from Base. in view of coming moves & ability to move on 4 Lorries	AJO
St Sixte	13/4/18		Moved to Sainte Sixte. Returned Stores not drawn by units to Base	AJO
	14/4/18		Received unserviceable & surplus stores from units & returned to Base	AJO
	15/4/18		6 Trench mortars received from Gun Park. reconsigned back to Base	AJO
	16/4/18		Travelling kitchen & 3 limbd G.S. wagons at Railhead wired units to clear,	AJO
	17/4/18		Moved to St Jan te Biezen.	AJO
St Jan te Biezen	18/4/18		Nothing to report. Visited Railhead in late afternoon.	AJO
	19/4/18		Heard that Division had moved to Bousseboom & under XXII Corps.	AJO

2353 Wt. W2544/1454 700,000 5/15 D. D. & L. A.D.S.S./Forms/C. 2118.

Instructions regarding War Diaries and Intelligence Summaries are contained in F. S. Regs., Part II. and the Staff Manual respectively. Title pages will be prepared in manuscript.

WAR DIARY
or
INTELLIGENCE SUMMARY. 2nd Sheet –

(*Erase heading not required.*)

Army Form C. 2118.

Place	Date	Hour	Summary of Events and Information	Remarks and references to Appendices
St Jan der Biezen	20/4/18		Visited Railhead & DHQ at Boussebourn	AM
			DAQMG. visited dump & office here.	
	21/4/18		Visited 89th & 21st Bde Staff Captains to enquire of actual urgent needs of units	AM
	22/4/18		Wire from 22 Corps transferring arty to me from II Anzac Corps. Sent 2 lorries to Calais	AM
	23/4/18		Visited DHQ at Boussebourn. Paid out Ordnance Detachment & attached personnel	AM
	24/4/18		Dump at St Jan der Biezen bombed by enemy. asked Q for fresh accomodation	AM
	25/4/18		moved to Brozeele. A.DOS. 22nd Corps visited dump & office	AM
	26/4/18		proceeded to Godwaersvelde to see W.O. in charge of Ord administr. of arty with VIII Corps	AM
Brozeele	27/4/18		proceeded to Calais. transferred to VIII Corps. Resumed issues from Base	AM
	28/4/18		Change of Railhead from Proven to ROUSBRUGGE. arranged forward dumps.	AM
	29/4/18		Transferred 21st & 89th Bdes to 21st Divn & Artillery to 22nd Corps Tps.	AM
	30/4/18			

1/5/18

[signature]
Major AOD
DADOS
30th Divn

#353 Wt. W2544/1454 700,000 5/15 D. D. & L. A.D.S.S./Forms/C. 2118.

Instructions regarding War Diaries and Intelligence Summaries are contained in F. S. Regs., Part II. and the Staff Manual respectively. Title pages will be prepared in manuscript.

WAR DIARY
or
INTELLIGENCE SUMMARY.
(Erase heading not required.)

Army Form C. 2118.

No 231

Place	Date	Hour	Summary of Events and Information	Remarks and references to Appendices
			Confidential	
			War Diary	
			of	
			D.A.D.O.S. 30th Div"	
			From 1st May 1918 to 31st May 1918	

2353 Wt W2544/1454 700,000 5/15 D. D. & L. A.D.S.S./Forms/C. 2118.

Instructions regarding War Diaries and Intelligence Summaries are contained in F. S. Regs., Part II. and the Staff Manual respectively. Title pages will be prepared in manuscript.

WAR DIARY
or
INTELLIGENCE SUMMARY.
(Erase heading not required.)

1st Sheet

Army Form C. 2118.

Place	Date	Hour	Summary of Events and Information	Remarks and references to Appendices
BROXEELE	1 5/18		Truck arrived at Railhead. cleared & stores issued to troops	APM
"	2 5/18		Visited XXII H.Qrs + advanced G office	APM
"	3 5/18		Visited Railhead.	APM
"	4 5/18		Truck arrived, cleared & stores issued to troops.	APM
"	5 5/18		No truck today. Railhead changed to PROVEN.	APM
"	6 5/18		Asst Insp. of armourers visited me. Railhead being shelled.	APM
"	7 5/18		Truck arrived at Railhead. cleared. Stores issued to troops	APM
"	8 5/18		No truck today. Visited Composite Bde H.Qrs	APM
"	9 5/18		Stores returned by units on disbandment sent to Base	APM
"	10 5/18		Truck arrived at Railhead, cleared & stores issued to troops	APM
"	11 5/18		Truck " " "	APM
"	12 5/18		Asst Inspr. of armourers visited me. Railhead change to ROUSBRUGGE.	APM
"	13 5/18		2 Trucks arrived at Railhead cleared. Stores issued to troops.	APM
"	14 5/18		Visited I.O.M. near St Omer.	APM
"	15 5/18		Visited St Omer for urgent local purchase	APM
"	16 5/18		Moved to EU. Suspended issues for 4 days.	APM
EU	17 5/18		Proceeded to 66th Divn to take over administration of 35th American Divn	APM
	18 5/18		Visited 66th Div DADOS together with 35th Am Div. Q.M. & D.O.O.	APM
	19 5/18		A.D.O.S. visited office	APM
	20 5/18		D.D.O.S. visited office	APM
	21 5/18		Visited 97th Field Ambce	APM
	22 5/18		Nothing of importance to report	APM
	23 5/18		Visited Railhead	APM
	24 5/18		Proceeded to M.T. Depot	APM
	25 5/18		Proceeded to ABBEVILLE	APM

2353 Wt. W2544/1454 700,000 5/15 D. D. & L. A.D.S.S./Forms/C. 2118.

Instructions regarding War Diaries and Intelligence Summaries are contained in F. S. Regs., Part II. and the Staff Manual respectively. Title pages will be prepared in manuscript.

WAR DIARY
or
INTELLIGENCE SUMMARY.
(Erase heading not required.)

2nd Sheet

Army Form C. 2118.

Place	Date	Hour	Summary of Events and Information	Remarks and references to Appendices
EU	26/5/18		notified that 33rd American Div will be administered by me.	AM
"	27/5/18		visited Railhead at WOINCOURT	AM
"	28/5/18		received notification that a DADOS will be attached for help in Equipment	AM
"	29/5/18		Visited 66th Div & proceeded with DADOS 66th Div to Abbeville	AM
"	30/5/18		GHQ Staff officer visited me to know how equipment of American Div is proceeding	AM
"	31/5/18		ADOS visited me	AM

A.P. Mummed[?]
Major
DADOS
30th Div

2353 Wt. W2544/1454 700,000 5/15 D. D. & L. A.D.S.S./Forms/C. 2118.

Instructions regarding War Diaries and Intelligence Summaries are contained in F. S. Regs., Part II. and the Staff Manual respectively. Title pages will be prepared in manuscript.

WAR DIARY
or
INTELLIGENCE SUMMARY.
(*Erase heading not required.*)

Army Form C. 2118.

Vol 32

Place	Date	Hour	Summary of Events and Information	Remarks and references to Appendices
			Confidential War Diary of D.A.D.O.S., 30th Div., From 1st June 1918 To 30th June 1918.	

2353 Wt. W2544/1454 700,000 5/15 D. D. & L. A.D.S.S./Forms/C. 2118.

Instructions regarding War Diaries and Intelligence Summaries are contained in F. S. Regs., Part II. and the Staff Manual respectively. Title pages will be prepared in manuscript.

WAR DIARY
or
INTELLIGENCE SUMMARY.
(Erase heading not required.)

1st Sheet

Army Form C. 2118.

Place	Date	Hour	Summary of Events and Information	Remarks and references to Appendices
EU	1/6/18		Visited Railhead & dump at Womcourt	AM
"	2/6/18		ADOS XIX Corps visited office	AM
"	3/6/18		DDOS Fourth Army visited office reference equipment of 35th American Division	AM
"	4/6/18		Capt V E Ward arrived from G.H.Q. to help in equipment of 33rd American Division	AM
"	5/6/18		Lieut C Hawkes arrived for a course of instruction in duties of DADOS	AM
"	6/6/18		35th American Division left to join French army	AM
"	7/6/18		Q.M.G., G.H.Q. visited office reference rifles ~~[illegible]~~ of 35th American & 33rd American Divn	AM
"	8/6/18		ADOS Fourth Army visited office	AM
"	9/6/18		Moved dump from St. Quentin to Womcourt	AM
"	10/6/18		ADOS XIX Corps visited office	AM
"	11/6/18		Visited dump & railhead at Womcourt.	AM
"	12/6/18		ADOS Fourth Army visited office	AM
"	13/6/18		Visited 33rd American Divisional Head Quarters	AM
"	14/6/18		Visited 97th Field Ambulance at Mesnilval	AM
"	15/6/18		Lieut C Hawkes left for Fourth Army Troops No1 to take over duties of Ordnance Officer	AM
"	16/6/18		Visited 21st Infy Bde Headquarters	AM
"	17/6/18		ADOS XIX Corps visited office	AM
"	18/6/18		33rd American Division transferred to 66th Division for completion of equipment & training	AM
"	19/6/18		Cadre battalions of 30th Division transferred to 66th Division	AM

2353 Wt. W2544/1454 700,000 5/15 D. D. & L. A.D.S.S./Forms/C. 2118.

Instructions regarding War Diaries and Intelligence Summaries are contained in F. S. Regs., Part II. and the Staff Manual respectively. Title pages will be prepared in manuscript.

WAR DIARY
or
INTELLIGENCE SUMMARY.
(*Erase heading not required.*)

2nd Sheet

Army Form C. 2118.

Place	Date	Hour	Summary of Events and Information	Remarks and references to Appendices
Eu	20		Moved to Rue	AM
Rue	21		Moved 5th Royal Irish Fusiliers to Lines of Communication. to be administered by 14th Div	AM
–	22		Visited C.O.O. Abbeville reference drawing of equipment of new Battns from Egypt	AM
–	23		Drew unit Equipment of 2/14 2/15 & 2/16 London Regiments & packed it on Rlwy Transport	AM
–	24		Visited Cast area to see if all Lewis & Vickers Guns had been returned to No 4 Gun Park	AM
–	25		Drew unit Equipment of 2/17 2/20 & 2/23 London Regiments	AM
–	26		Drew unit Equipment of 2/24 London Regiment. 6th Dublin Fus & 5th Inniskilling Fus.	AM
–	27		Moved to Eperlecques. now in VII Corps Second Army	AM
Eperlecques	28		A.D.O.S. VII Corps visited office	AM
–	29		Nothing to report. Received new bulk programme from C.O.O. Calais	AM
–	30		Visited Railhead A.D.O.S. called at the office.	AM

A M Newell [signature]
Major A.O.D.
D.A.D.O.S. 30th Div.

2353 Wt. W2544/1454 700,000 5/15 D. D. & L. A.D.S.S./Forms/C. 2118.

Army Form C. 2118.

Instructions regarding War Diaries and Intelligence Summaries are contained in F. S. Regs., Part II. and the Staff Manual respectively. Title pages will be prepared in manuscript.

WAR DIARY
or
INTELLIGENCE SUMMARY.

(Erase heading not required.)

WO 33

Place	Date	Hour	Summary of Events and Information	Remarks and references to Appendices
			Confidential	
			War Diary	
			of	
			D.A.D.O.S.	
			30th Divn	
			From 1st July 1918 To 31st July 1918.	

2353 Wt. W2544/1454 700,000 5/15 D. D. & L. A.D.S.S./Forms/C. 2118.

Instructions regarding War Diaries and Intelligence Summaries are contained in F. S. Regs., Part II. and the Staff Manual respectively. Title pages will be prepared in manuscript.

WAR DIARY
or
INTELLIGENCE SUMMARY.
(Erase heading not required.)

1st Sheet

Army Form C. 2118.

Place	Date	Hour	Summary of Events and Information	Remarks and references to Appendices
Eperlecques	1/7/18		ADOS visited Office	[illegible]
"	2/7/18		Proceeded to Watten Railhead	[illegible]
"	3/7/18		Visited 2nd South Lancashire Regiment at Bayenghem	[illegible]
"	4/7/18		Visited 2/17th London Regiment at Ouesmont	[illegible]
"	5/7/18		Went to Railhead	[illegible]
"	6/7/18		Visited 2/14th London Scottish London Regiment at Serques	[illegible]
"	7/7/18		Visited 2/15th London Regiment at Moulle	[illegible]
"	8/7/18		Moved to ~~[illegible]~~ Cassel	[illegible]
Cassel	9/7/18		Visited 2/16th London Regiment at Les Marnières	[illegible]
"	10/7/18		A.D.O.S. visited office with Corps Salvage officer.	[illegible]
"	11/7/18		Visited 7/8th Inniskilling Fusiliers at Wisbrove	[illegible]
"	12/7/18		Visited 7th Irish Regiment at Hellebrouck	[illegible]
"	13/7/18		Visited 30th Bn Machine Gun Corps.	[illegible]
"	14/7/18		Visited 2/23rd London Regiment	[illegible]
"	15/7/18		Visited South Wales Borders (Pioneers)	[illegible]
"	16/7/18		Visited 1/6 Cheshire Regiment.	[illegible]
"	17/7/18		Conference at DHQ	[illegible]
"	18/7/18		D.D.O.S. & A.D.O.S. visited office & inspected Dump.	[illegible]
"	19/7/18		Visited 98th Field Ambulance.	[illegible]

2353 Wt. W2544/1454 700,000 5/15 D. D. & L. A.D.S.S./Forms/C. 2118.

Instructions regarding War Diaries and Intelligence Summaries are contained in F. S. Regs., Part II. and the Staff Manual respectively. Title pages will be prepared in manuscript.

WAR DIARY
or
INTELLIGENCE SUMMARY.
(*Erase heading not required.*)

2nd Sheet.

Army Form C. 2118.

Place	Date	Hour	Summary of Events and Information	Remarks and references to Appendices
Cassel	20/7/18		Visited 89th Bde HQrs	AM
"	21/7/18		Visited 200 Field Company	AM
"	22/7/18		Proceeded to Calais Base - now removed to Vendroux.	AM
"	23/7/18		Visited 21st Bde HQrs.	AM
"	24/7/18		Visited HQrs & No 1 Coy Train.	AM
"	25/7/18		Proceeded to Railhead.	AM
"	26/7/18		Proceeded to Calais to get samples & quotations for Divisional Badge.	AM
"	27/7/18		ADOS visited office & dump.	AM
"	28/7/18		Nothing to report of importance.	AM
"	29/7/18		Corps Ammunition Officer visited me	AM
"	30/7/18		Visited Calais to order Divisional Badge.	AM
"	31/7/18		Railhead Ordnance Officer visited me	AM

A M Munro[?] Major
DADOS
30th Divn.
1/8/18.

4

Instructions regarding War Diaries and Intelligence Summaries are contained in F. S. Regs., Part II. and the Staff Manual respectively. Title pages will be prepared in manuscript.

WAR DIARY
or
INTELLIGENCE SUMMARY.
(*Erase heading not required.*)

Army Form C. 2118.

3

Vol 34

Place	Date	Hour	Summary of Events and Information	Remarks and references to Appendices
			Confidential War Diary of D.A.D.O.S. 50th Divn From 1st Aug 1918 To 31st Aug 1918.	

2353 Wt. W2544/1454 700,000 5/15 D. D. & L. A.D.S.S./Forms/C. 2118.

Instructions regarding War Diaries and Intelligence Summaries are contained in F. S. Regs., Part II. and the Staff Manual respectively. Title pages will be prepared in manuscript.

WAR DIARY
or
INTELLIGENCE SUMMARY.
(Erase heading not required.)

1st Sheet

Army Form C. 2118.

Place	Date	Hour	Summary of Events and Information	Remarks and references to Appendices
Cassel	1/8/18		Visited Railhead and arranged re. u/s	
	2		Two trucks arrived. Cleared and distributed	
	3		Nothing of importance	
	4		ADOS called during morning. Inspected dump. All in order.	
	5		Truck of Clothing at Railhead	
	6		Obtained car for purpose of finding suitable refilling Point.	
	7		Truck arrived and stores sent to Refilling Point.	
	8		Divisional H.Q moved to TERDEGHEM. My store remains at Cassel	
	9		Visited DHQ reference special stores required for operations.	
	10		Obtained car for purpose of purchasing Luminous Paint. No success.	
	11		Again tried to get Luminous Paint but learned it was unobtainable by Lt.	
	12		Trucks (2) arrived at Railhead. Cleared by noon.	
	13		Stores taken to Refilling Point	
	14		Visited by ADOS who looked through office records	
	15		Visited Wagon Lines of several Units. Position re. Ordnance Stores quite satisfactory	
	16		Truck of Clothing at Railhead	
	17		Moved my office to 17 Rue de Bergues in order to be nearer to dump.	
	18		DOAMG visited dump. Sent urgent operation stores to Units.	
	19		Purchased some Lamps for use of D.H.Q in advanced positions (dug outs)	
	20		Delivered lamps to advanced DHQ. Truck arrived at Railhead.	
	21		Refilled Units at Refilling Point.	
	22		Visited Railhead; saw RCO and R.T.O.	

2353 Wt. W2544/1454 700,000 5/15 D. D. & L. A.D.S.S./Forms/C. 2118.

7

Instructions regarding War Diaries and Intelligence Summaries are contained in F. S. Regs., Part II. and the Staff Manual respectively. Title pages will be prepared in manuscript.

WAR DIARY
or
~~INTELLIGENCE SUMMARY.~~
(Erase heading not required.)

2nd Sheet — Army Form C. 2118.

Place	Date	Hour	Summary of Events and Information	Remarks and references to Appendices
Cassel	23/8		A/Major Roberts ~~[illegible]~~ arrived to relieve me closed my imprest a/c preparatory to leaving	
"	24/8		Took over Ordnance Officer Duty from Major Stewart at Cassel was interviewed by AA & QMG & DAQMG at 30th Divisional HQ Terdeghem	
"	25/8		General Routine Major Stewart left to take over 14th Divisional Ordnance	
"	26/8		6 Tons of Stores at Railhead	
"	27/8		Visited Refilling Point interviewed the Quartermasters of Battalions General Routine	
"	28/8		Visited Ammunition Dump & Bomb Store with DAQMG	
"	29/8		6 Tons of Stores at Railhead drawing 12 Lewis Guns daily from Battalions for inspection & on return drawing 12 others for inspection	
	[illegible]/8		Visited refilling point saw distribution of stores afternoon in office Dump	
	[illegible]/8		General Routine Received orders to move forward Division afternoon to Godewaersvelde early in the morning	

H Leonard Roberts Major
DADOS 30 Division

#353 Wt. W2544/1454 700,000 5/15 D. D. & L. A.D.S.S./Forms/C. 2118.

Instructions regarding War Diaries and Intelligence Summaries are contained in F. S. Regs., Part II. and the Staff Manual respectively. Title pages will be prepared in manuscript.

WAR DIARY
or
INTELLIGENCE SUMMARY.
(Erase heading not required.)

Army Form C. 2118.

Vol 35

Place	Date	Hour	Summary of Events and Information	Remarks and references to Appendices
			[illegible]	

2353 Wt. W2544/1454 700,000 5/15 D. D. & L. A.D.S.S./Forms/C 2118.

Instructions regarding War Diaries and Intelligence Summaries are contained in F. S. Regs., Part II. and the Staff Manual respectively. Title pages will be prepared in manuscript.

WAR DIARY
or
~~INTELLIGENCE SUMMARY.~~
(Erase heading not required.)

Army Form C. 2118.

1st Sheet

Place	Date	Hour	Summary of Events and Information	Remarks and references to Appendices
Godewaersvelde	1/9/18		Moving up from Cassel	
"	2/9/18		4 Tons of Stores at Railhead completed the move from Cassel to Godewaersvelde	
"	3/9/18		Units refilled with all available stores at Westoutre Church General Routine	
"	4/9/18		Visited Salvage Dump collected all Ordnance Stores General Routine	
"	5/9/18		7 Tons of Stores at Railhead	
"	6/9/18		Visited refilling point visited RMS stores of 2/23 London Regt 2/7 London Regt all correct	
"	7/9/18		General Routine	
"	8/9/18		Visited Refilling Point 189th Brigade delivered Hot Food Containers Water Carrying Packs roads in a very bad condition forward	
"	9/9/18		6 Tons of Stores at railhead started Tailors making Flaps for Box respirators for signalling to aeroplanes	
"	10/9/18		General Routine	
"	11/9/18		Visited Salvage Dumps General Routine	
"	12/9/18		General Routine	

8353 Wt. W2544/1454 700,000 5/15 D. D. & L. A.D.S.S./Forms/C. 2118.

Instructions regarding War Diaries and Intelligence Summaries are contained in F. S. Regs., Part II. and the Staff Manual respectively. Title pages will be prepared in manuscript.

WAR DIARY
or
~~INTELLIGENCE~~ SUMMARY.
(Erase heading not required.)

2nd Sheet

Army Form C. 2118.

Place	Date	Hour	Summary of Events and Information	Remarks and references to Appendices
[illegible]	13/9/18		Visited Refilling Point & [illegible] [illegible] Regt 90 Brigade & [illegible] Regt all correct. General Routine	
	14/9/18		General Routine	
	15/9/18		Visited Salvage Dump. Gas Officer regarding Gas Stores taken over the trenches	
	16/9/18		Went to Calais arranging a quotation [illegible] for 30th Divisional [illegible]	
	17/9/18		General Routine	
	18/9/18		General Routine	
	19/9/18		[illegible] of stores at Railhead [illegible] Salvage Dump R.E.C.	
	20/9/18		85 [illegible] Bottles at Railhead [illegible] Refilling Point [illegible] [illegible] [illegible] [illegible] [illegible] [illegible] [illegible] [illegible] Rest	
	21/9/18		Clearing [illegible] [illegible] consignment of [illegible]	
	22/9/18		Clearing [illegible] consignment of [illegible] Bottles [illegible]	
	23/9/18		Refilling [illegible] [illegible] Bottles to Brigades	
	24/9/18		Went to Calais to purchase lamps urgently required by Division [illegible] [illegible] [illegible]	
	25/9/18		[illegible] [illegible] sets of [illegible] Bottles at Railhead	

2353 Wt. W2544/1454 700,000 5/15 D. D. & L. A.D.S.S./Forms/C. 2118.

Instructions regarding War Diaries and Intelligence Summaries are contained in F. S. Regs., Part II. and the Staff Manual respectively. Title pages will be prepared in manuscript.

WAR DIARY
or
~~INTELLIGENCE SUMMARY.~~ 3rd Sheet.

(Erase heading not required.)

Army Form C. 2118.

Place	Date	Hour	Summary of Events and Information	Remarks and references to Appendices
Godewaersvelde	26/9/18		130 sets of Tent Bottoms & 6 Tons of Stores at Railhead for Distribution	
	27/9/18		Went to Cassel to obtain Boxes & Ribbons required for the Division. Busy issuing Tent Bottoms etc General Routine 7 Tons of Stores at Railhead	
	28/9/18		55 Sets of Tent Bottoms at Railhead	
	29/9/18		80 sets of Tent Bottoms at Railhead in the afternoon proceeded to Westoutre looking for a suitable Dump not much success called at Division H.Q. talked matters over with DARMG	
	30/9/18		Railhead changed to Ouderdom visited Railhead 6 Tons of Stores Train 5 hours late	

H Leonard Roberts Lieut
DADOS
30th Division

2353 Wt. W2544/1454 700,000 5/15 D. D. & L. A.D.S.S./Forms/C. 2118.

Vol 36

Confidential

War Diary

of

C.R.A.S.

30th British Division

From 1st October 1918 To 31st October 1918

Instructions regarding War Diaries and Intelligence Summaries are contained in F. S. Regs., Part II. and the Staff Manual respectively. Title pages will be prepared in manuscript.

WAR DIARY

or

INTELLIGENCE SUMMARY.

(Erase heading not required.)

Army Form C. 2118.

1st Sheet

Place	Date	Hour	Summary of Events and Information	Remarks and references to Appendices
Godewaersvelde	1/10/18		Visited the La Clytte Kemmel Road to look for a Dump. The Road to Kemmel be impossible I decided to make the Dump at La Clytte	
La Clytte	2/10/18		Moved Office & part of Stores to La Clytte. Putting up Store Tents after filling in shellholes	
"	3rd		Settling down. Bringing forward balance of Stores from Godewaersvelde went to Division to see AA & QMG endeavouring to be put on the Telephone to Divisional HQ	
"	4		4 Trucks of Stores winter clothing at Railhead still clearing old Dump making shelters at new location	
"	5		Refilling units. Bringing up Tent Bottoms from old location	
"	6		Went to DHQ Kemmel to find a sight for the Office so as to be nearer Division HQ in communication on the Telephone 6 Trucks of Winter clothing very heavy day	
"	7		Found a suitable site at Kemmel putting up a hut in preparation for moving there as soon as the roads are satisfactory for transport	
"	8		Visited Kemmel to see how the work is progressing roads in a very bad state of repair wet slippery	
"	9		General Routine. Visited refilling point in the morning	
"	10		Visited Kemmel in the morning process of clearing ground & putting up shelter progressing very slowly for want of labour. Went to [illegible] in the evening brought back [illegible] Capt. Gillespie [illegible] operations	

Instructions regarding War Diaries and Intelligence Summaries are contained in F. S. Regs., Part II. and the Staff Manual respectively. Title pages will be prepared in manuscript.

WAR DIARY
or
INTELLIGENCE SUMMARY.
(Erase heading not required.)

Army Form C. 2118.

2nd Sheet

Place	Date	Hour	Summary of Events and Information	Remarks and references to Appendices
[illegible]	11/X/18		General Routine 4 Tons of Stores at Railhead	
	[illegible]/X/18		Hut finished ready for use moved stock of Gas Stores to Kemmel straightening out ground for store tents	
"	[illegible]/X/18		General Routine 8 Tons at Railhead	
	14/X/18		Went to Kemmel & Wytschaete met AA&QMG on the way arranged to postpone move to Kemmel pending further developments	
	[illegible]/X/18		General Routine.	
"	15/X/18		General Routine looking for a site for a new Dump round St Eloi [illegible] could find nothing at all suitable	
"	[illegible]/X/18		Field Cashier for Pay. Sent away 500 Pairs Gum Boots	
	18/X/18		Moving up to Basse [illegible] District	
	19/10/18		Selected suitable site at Q27 near WERVICQ for dump. Railhead changes to DE KENNEBAK	
Wervicq (Q.27)	20/10/18		Commenced move. Owing to distance unable to complete move. Visited DHQ at [illegible]	
	21/10/18		Completed move. Visited DHQ at STERHOEK Railhead no change. 3 lorries under repairs	
	22/10/18		6 Trucks at DE KENNEBAK Railhead. One lorry to clear. Two trucks cleared, [illegible] one dump at siding. RTO [illegible] 4 back to Base. DAQMG visited dump.	
	23/10/18		ADOS visited dump. Lorries sent to clear Railhead siding. Visited DHQ. Selected suitable site for dump STERHOEK	

8353 Wt. W2544/1454 700,000 5/15 D. D. & L. A.D.S.S./Forms/C. 2118.

Army Form C. 2118.

Instructions regarding War Diaries and Intelligence Summaries are contained in F. S. Regs., Part II. and the Staff Manual respectively. Title Pages will be prepared in manuscript.

WAR DIARY
or
INTELLIGENCE SUMMARY

(Erase heading not required.)

3rd Sheet.

Place	Date	Hour	Summary of Events and Information	Remarks and references to Appendices
WERVICQ (Q 27)	24/10/18		Moved to STERHOEK. Partly completed move. Visited DAQMG	
STERHOEK	25/10/18		Completed move. Units drawing stores rapidly. Take over administration of Divl Clothing Store.	
	26/10/18		Lorries sent to DE KENNEBAK Railhead. Truck vehicles and truck General Stores. Dumped one lorry load with guard, unable to clear on lorries	
	27/10/18		Cleared remaining load stores from Railhead to other trucks. Salved Travelling Kitchen and Water Cart from back area. Delivered to Workshops.	
	28/10/18		Truck vehicles Railhead. ADOS visited office. No complaints.	
	29/10/18		Railhead changes to MENIN. Two trucks in. Delivered clean clothing to Units in the Line	
	30/10/18		Two trucks General stores Railhead. Cleared and distributed. Quantities area stores returned to Corps and Army Troops.	
	31/10/18		Two trucks underclothing for Laundry at Railhead. Cleared to Clothing Store. General routine.	

H Leonard Roberts
Major
DADOS 30th Brit Division

2449 Wt. W14957/M90 750,000 1/16 J.B.C. & A. Forms/C.2118/12.

9837

Confidential

War Diary

of

ADMS 30th British Division

From 1st November 1918 to 30 November 1918

Instructions regarding War Diaries and Intelligence Summaries are contained in F. S. Regs., Part II. and the Staff Manual respectively. Title pages will be prepared in manuscript.

WAR DIARY
or
~~INTELLIGENCE~~ SUMMARY.
(Erase heading not required.)

1st Sheet

Army Form C. 2118.

Place	Date	Hour	Summary of Events and Information	Remarks and references to Appendices
Stedhoek	1/11/18		Two Trucks of Stores reconsigned from last area. Two Trucks of General Stores. All cleared. Despatched Truck [illegible] underclothing to Army Laundry	
"	2/11/18		One Truck at Railhead. Units drawing very well. Decided with D.A.Q.M.G. to refill Units of 2 Brigades at advanced Refilling Point.	
"	3/11/18		3 Lorry loads of unserviceable sent to Railhead. 3 Trucks cleared. 1 Lorry refilling 2nd 18th Brigades. Endeavoured to find a Store at Belleghem but unsuccessful	
Belleghem	4/11/18		Decided to move Dump to Rolleghem. Moved Office to Belleghem. Dump to Rolleghem.	
"	5/11/18		Completed move from Stedhoek to Rolleghem. Sent away all underclothing [illegible] laundry for replacement. Informed by R at 9.30pm we must move the Dump at Rolleghem to Belleghem by noon tomorrow as it is out of our area.	
	6/11/18		Found suitable Dump at Belleghem. Cleared Railhead moved a considerable amount of Stores to new Dump.	
	7/11/18		Completing move. Armourers, Shoemakers, Tailors shops, clean clothing store to new area, making distribution of bulk stores received from Railhead yesterday.	
	8/11/18		Visited Railhead, Salvage Dump, reconsigned Truck of Laundry from Menin to new Railhead. Visited Q.M. Stores of 7th Royal Irish Regt.	

2353 Wt. W2544/1454 700,000 5/15 D. D. & L. A.D.S.S./Forms/C. 2118.

Army Form C. 2118.

Instructions regarding War Diaries and Intelligence Summaries are contained in F. S. Regs., Part II. and the Staff Manual respectively. Title Pages will be prepared in manuscript.

WAR DIARY
or
INTELLIGENCE SUMMARY

(Erase heading not required.)

2nd Sheet

Place	Date	Hour	Summary of Events and Information	Remarks and references to Appendices
Belleghem	[illegible]/18		General Routine	
	[illegible]		Visited new Railhead at Courtrai 6 Tons of stores there all cleared	
	[illegible]		Went to Divisional Head Quarters at Heestert. [illegible] does not [illegible] Ordnance Officer [illegible] at present saw Staff Capt 90th Brigade no complaints	
	[illegible]		Visited Railhead at Sweveghem saw the R.T.O. with reference to supplies [illegible] [illegible] for the present from the [illegible]	
	[illegible]		Went to [illegible] Corps [illegible] obtained 20 Pairs of Gum Boots [illegible] [illegible] for Battery [illegible] 6 Tons of stores at Railhead [illegible]	
	[illegible]		Refilling [illegible] at Heestert [illegible] [illegible] [illegible] to the Church at Heestert [illegible] to complete refilling [illegible]	
	[illegible]		[illegible] [illegible] all stores [illegible] to Belleghem	
	[illegible]		[illegible] for [illegible] [illegible] General Routine	
	[illegible]		[illegible] of Stores at Railhead [illegible]	
	[illegible]		[illegible] of Stores at Railhead [illegible]	
	[illegible]		General Routine	
	[illegible]		[illegible] Tons of General Stores at Railhead all cleared	

2449 Wt. W14957/M90 750,000 1/16 J.B.C. & A. Forms/C.2118/12.

Army Form C. 2118.

Instructions regarding War Diaries and Intelligence Summaries are contained in F. S. Regs., Part II. and the Staff Manual respectively. Title Pages will be prepared in manuscript.

WAR DIARY
or
INTELLIGENCE SUMMARY

(Erase heading not required.)

3rd Sheet

Place	Date	Hour	Summary of Events and Information	Remarks and references to Appendices
Belleghem	21/11/18		General Routine Units drawing well	
"	22/11/18		1000 Blankets advised at Railhead Train very late in arriving waited at Railhead from 3pm until 9pm. Brought back 5 lorry loads	
"	23/11/18		5 Tons of General Stores at Railhead in addition to the Balance of Blankets all cleared All Blankets in possession of Units by evening	
"	24/11/18		General Routine	
"	25/11/18		8 Tons of Stores at Railhead All cleared Interviewed several Quartermasters	
"	26/11/18		Additional 1000 Blankets at Railhead	
"	27/11/18		Sent 2 lorries to Q 28 Central to clear Balance of Tent Bottoms Trench Shelters	
"	28/11/18		Reconsigned 2 trucks to new Railhead at Aire preparing to move to new Area.	
Blaringhem	29/11/18		Started from Belleghem at 7.30 am called at St Andre & saw the R.T.O. explained to him we could not come back & asked him to reconsign any trucks arriving for D.A.D.O.S. to Aire arrived at Blaringhem 3.30pm arranged Office Billets	
"	30/11/18		Balance of Stores from old Dump arrived visit of Aire Railhead no stores yet.	

H Leonard Roberts Major DADOS 30 British Division

2449 Wt. W14957/M90 750,000 1/16 J.B.C. & A. Forms/C.2118/12.

VR 38

Confidential

War Diary

of

ERRTS 30th British Division

From 1st December 1918. To 31st December 1918

Army Form C. 2118.

Instructions regarding War Diaries and Intelligence Summaries are contained in F. S. Regs., Part II. and the Staff Manual respectively. Title Pages will be prepared in manuscript.

WAR DIARY
or
~~INTELLIGENCE~~ SUMMARY

(Erase heading not required.)

1st Sheet

Place	Date	Hour	Summary of Events and Information	Remarks and references to Appendices
1918 Blaringhem	1 Dec		Visited Railhead no stores Assisting D.E.C. Salvage etc arriving in this area today	
"	2/12/18		6 Trucks of stores at Railhead all cleared brought to the Dump balance of stores at Belleghem brought to Blaringhem	
"	3/12/18 to 6/12/18		General Routine	
	7/12/18 to 8/12/18		General Routine	
	9/12/18		4 Tons of Stores at Railhead	
	10/12/18		Visited Divisional HQ no difficulties	
	11/12/18		Visited R.E. Dump at Renescure obtained some iron wire for caps all that was obtainable 3 Tons of stores at Railhead	
	12/12/18 13/12/18 14/12/18		General Routine	
	15/12/18		Visited Railhead Wagon Cable there for Div Signal Coy	
	16/12/18		General Routine	
	17/12/18		Visited Railhead 4 Tons of General Stores	

2449 Wt. W14957/M90 750,000 1/16 J.B.C. & A. Forms/C.2118/12.

Instructions regarding War Diaries and Intelligence Summaries are contained in F. S. Regs., Part II. and the Staff Manual respectively. Title Pages will be prepared in manuscript.

WAR DIARY
or
~~INTELLIGENCE SUMMARY~~

(Erase heading not required.)

Army Form C. 2118.

2nd Sheet

Place	Date	Hour	Summary of Events and Information	Remarks and references to Appendices
1918 [illegible]			General Routine	
"	[illegible]			
"	[illegible]		4 Tons of Stores at Railhead [illegible] 1000 Blankets	
"	[illegible]		General Routine	
"	[illegible]		Visited [illegible] Regt [illegible] also Railhead	
"	[illegible]		400 [illegible] 6 Tons of General Stores at Railhead [illegible]	
"	[illegible]		3 Tons of Stores at Railhead	
"	[illegible]		General Routine	
"	[illegible]			
"	[illegible]		225 Tables 400 [illegible] at Railhead also 6 Tons of General Stores [illegible]	
"	[illegible]		General Routine	
"	[illegible]		5 Tons of [illegible] General Stores at Railhead	
"	[illegible]		General Routine	
"	[illegible]		5 Tons of General Stores at Railhead	
"	[illegible]		General Routine	

[illegible signature]

2449 Wt. W14957/M90 750,000 1/16 J.B.C. & A. Forms/C.2118/12.

30

VR 39

Confidential

War Diary

of

DADOS

30th British Division

From 1st January 1919 to 31st January 1919

Army Form C. 2118.

Instructions regarding War Diaries and Intelligence Summaries are contained in F. S. Regs., Part II. and the Staff Manual respectively. Title Pages will be prepared in manuscript.

WAR DIARY
or
~~INTELLIGENCE SUMMARY~~

(Erase heading not required.)

1st Sheet

Place	Date	Hour	Summary of Events and Information	Remarks and references to Appendices
1919				
Blaringhem	1/1/19		The question of Boots having become serious the matter has been taken up with ADOS XIX Corps & the DADRT asked to try & trace a truck some days overdue this has been done & should be at Railhead tomorrow	
	2/1/19		4 Tons of General Stores & Lumber, RT at Railhead	
	3/1/19		The question of Nosebags & non arrival of same taken up with ADOS with a view to expediting. He states there is a general shortage throughout the Army	
	4/1/19		General Routine	
	5/1/19		General Routine	
	6/1/19		Went to Divisional HQ with reference to the [illegible] of Brigades which going down to the coast.	
	7/1/19		3000 Blankets at Railhead & 6 tons of General Stores. [illegible] 4 9th Brigade [illegible] to Etaples having to stay & bring them back in 3 days time when the Brigade has settled down in the new area	
	8/1/19		General Routine	
	9/1/19		5 Tons of General Stores at Railhead. A large consignment of unserviceable dispatched to the Base	
	10/1/19		WO Clerk & Foreman return from Etaples after delivering the Stores	

2449 Wt. W14957/M90 750,000 1/16 J.B.C. & A. Forms/C.2118/12.

Instructions regarding War Diaries and Intelligence Summaries are contained in F. S. Regs., Part II. and the Staff Manual respectively. Title Pages will be prepared in manuscript.

WAR DIARY
or
~~INTELLIGENCE SUMMARY~~

(Erase heading not required.)

Army Form C. 2118.

2nd Sheet

Place	Date	Hour	Summary of Events and Information	Remarks and references to Appendices
Blaringhem	11/1/19		General Routine	
	12/1/19 – 13/1/19		General Routine	
	14/1/19		3 Tons of Stores at Railhead	
	15/1/19		Two Warrant Officers sent for Temporary Duty to 5th Army HQ	
	16/1/19 to 23/1/19		General Routine	
	24/1/19		Visited Area Commandants, inspected Dumps, & clearing all surplus Ordnance Stores to Corps Troops & Base	
	25/1/19		Visited Railhead & Head Quarters of 148 & 149 Arty Bdges regarding Service Dress with a view to cutting down demands	
	26/1/19 to 28/1/19		General Routine	
	29/1/19		Visited Aire with a view to obtaining a suitable Dump under the scheme for a Intermediate Collecting Station	
	30/1/19		Visited Railhead Brigade & No 1 Coy Divisional Train	
	31/1/19		Decided on a suitable Store for an Intermediate Collecting Station	

H Leonard Roberts Major
DADVS. 30th [illegible] Division

2449 Wt. W14957/M90 750,000 1/16 J.B.C. & A. Forms/C.2118/12.

4 30

VR 40

Confidential

War Diary

of

D.A.D.V.S.

30th British Division

From 1st Feby 1919 To 28th Feb, 1919

Army Form C. 2118.

Instructions regarding War Diaries and Intelligence Summaries are contained in F. S. Regs., Part II. and the Staff Manual respectively. Title Pages will be prepared in manuscript.

WAR DIARY

or

~~INTELLIGENCE SUMMARY~~

(Erase heading not required.)

1st Sheet

Place	Date	Hour	Summary of Events and Information	Remarks and references to Appendices
1919 Blaringhem	1/2/19		Reported to ADVS site selected for Intermediate Collecting Station	
	2/2/19		Visited Railhead no stores yet received	
	3/2/19		General Routine	
	4/2/19		3 Tons of General Stores at Railhead	
	5/2/19		General Routine	
	6/2/19		Heavy snow fall considerable demand for boots in consequence supply sufficient to meet all demands.	
	7/2/19		General Routine	
	8/2/19		4 Tons of General Stores at Railhead	
	9/2/19		Visited DAC at Bailleul took up boots clothing urgently needed in the cas[e] Went thoroughly into the difficulties with them & arranged for future requirements	
	10/2/19 &	11/2/19	General Routine	
	12/2/19		Visited Railhead & RTO with regard to missing trucks	
	14/2/19		3 Tons of General Stores at Railhead	
	15/2/19 &	16/2/19	General Routine.	

Instructions regarding War Diaries and Intelligence Summaries are contained in F. S. Regs., Part II. and the Staff Manual respectively. Title Pages will be prepared in manuscript.

WAR DIARY
or
INTELLIGENCE SUMMARY

(Erase heading not required.)

Army Form C. 2118.

2nd Sheet

Place	Date	Hour	Summary of Events and Information	Remarks and references to Appendices
Blaringhem	17/1/19	20/1/19	General Routine	
"	21/1/19		ADOS XIX Corps informs me of the death of Major W H Swallow & orders me to proceed to St Omer & take over DADOS duties 31st Division. Went to St Omer & arranged to go & stay the next morning	
St Omer	22/1/19		Taking over duties ADOS & DADOS visited Office closed Imprest account for the time being	
"	23/1/19		Visited RAH Ordnance Units in the area belonging to 31 Division	
"	24/1/19		" " XIX Corps regarding return of stores &c	
"	25/1/19		General Routine	
"	26/1/19		" " visited Blaringhem to see how my own Ordnance was functioning	
"	27/1/19		General Routine	
"	28/1/19		" " 7 Trucks containing 31 Army Supply Column surplus Stores despatched to Beaumarais	

H Leonard Roberts Major
DADOS 30th Division

2449 Wt. W14957/M90 750,000 1/16 J.B.C. & A. Forms/C.2118/12.

Army Form C. 2118.

WAR DIARY
or
INTELLIGENCE SUMMARY.

(Erase heading not required.)

Instructions regarding War Diaries and Intelligence Summaries are contained in F. S. Regs., Part II. and the Staff Manual respectively. Title pages will be prepared in manuscript.

Place	Date	Hour	Summary of Events and Information	Remarks and references to Appendices
Headquarters, Ostrohove Camp, BOULOGNE.	March 1st to 31st, 1919.		Weather intermittently fine and showery ending with a short spell of cold stormy weather.	
			The Brigade continued to be employed on Demobilization duties at BOULOGNE. A total of 2,233 Officers and 69,441 O.R.s for Demobilization from 1st, 3rd and 5th Armies and L. of C. Area, passed through the Camps administered by the Brigade during the month.	
			One Company of 2/17th Bn. London Regiment were employed on guarding supply trains, and details of the Battalion on P. of W. Escorts.	
			Brigadier-General WALLACE WRIGHT, V.C., C.M.G., D.S.O., assumed command of the Brigade on 22nd inst., vice Brigadier-General R.A.M.CURRIE, C.M.G., D.S.O., on his appointment to command a Brigade of the Army of the Rhine..	

TOTAL RE-INFORCEMENTS RECEIVED DURING THE MONTH OF MARCH:-

	Officers.	O.R.
7/8th Bn. R. Inniskilling Fusiliers.	30	488.
1/5th Bn. South Lancashire Regt.	11	322
2/17th Bn. London Regt.	19	233
	60.	1,043

TOTAL PERSONNEL DEMOBILISED FROM THE BRIGADE DURING THE MONTH OF MARCH:-

	Officers.	O.R.
Brigade H.Q. & L.T.M.B.		20.
7/8th Bn. R. Inniskilling Fusiliers.	10	175
1/5th Bn. S. Lancashire Regt	5	101
2/17th Bn. London Regiment.	7	122
	22.	418

[signature] Capt for Brigadier General,
Commanding 89th Infantry Brigade.

D. D. & L., London, E.C.
(A10206) Wt W5300/P713 750,000 2/18 Sch. 52 Forms/C2118/16

www.ingramcontent.com/pod-product-compliance
Lightning Source LLC
Chambersburg PA
CBHW081412160426
43193CB00013B/2158

* 9 7 8 1 4 7 4 5 1 5 1 1 5 *